ONE BIG TENT

Atheist and agnostic AA members share their
experience, strength and hope

T0151781

BOOKS PUBLISHED BY AA GRAPEVINE, INC.

The Language of the Heart (& eBook)
The Best of the Grapevine Volume I (eBook only)
The Best of Bill (& eBook)
Thank You for Sharing
Spiritual Awakenings (& eBook)
I Am Responsible: The Hand of AA
The Home Group: Heartbeat of AA (& eBook)
Emotional Sobriety — The Next Frontier (& eBook)
Spiritual Awakenings II (& eBook)
In Our Own Words: Stories of Young AAs in Recovery (& eBook)
Beginners' Book (& eBook)
Voices of Long-Term Sobriety (& eBook)
A Rabbit Walks Into A Bar
Step by Step — Real AAs, Real Recovery (& eBook)
Emotional Sobriety II — The Next Frontier (& eBook)
Young & Sober (& eBook)
Into Action (& eBook)
Happy, Joyous & Free (& eBook)
One on One (& eBook)
No Matter What (& eBook)
Grapevine Daily Quote Book (& eBook)
Sober & Out (& eBook)
Forming True Partnerships (& eBook)
Our Twelve Traditions (& eBook)
Making Amends (& eBook)
Voices of Women in AA (& eBook)
AA in the Military (& eBook)

IN SPANISH
El lenguaje del corazón
Lo mejor de Bill (& eBook)
El grupo base: Corazón de AA
Lo mejor de La Viña
Felices, alegres y libres (& eBook)
Un día a la vez (& eBook)
Frente A Frente (& eBook)

IN FRENCH
Le langage du coeur
Les meilleurs articles de Bill
Le Groupe d'attache: Le battement du coeur des AA
En tête à tête (& eBook)
Heureux, joyeux et libres (& eBook)

ONE BIG TENT

Atheist and agnostic AA members share their
experience, strength and hope

AAGRAPEVINE,Inc.
New York, New York
WWW. AAGRAPEVINE.ORG

AA PREAMBLE

Alcoholics Anonymous is a fellowship of men and women
who share their experience, strength and hope
with each other that they may solve their common problem
and help others to recover from alcoholism.

The only requirement for membership is a desire to stop drinking.
There are no dues or fees for AA membership;
we are self-supporting through our own contributions.
AA is not allied with any sect, denomination, politics, organization
or institution; does not wish to engage in any controversy,
neither endorses nor opposes any causes.

Our primary purpose is to stay sober
and help other alcoholics to achieve sobriety.

© *AA Grapevine, Inc.*

CONTENTS

CHAPTER ONE

Staying Sober—No Matter What

Atheists share how they work the program, one day at a time

CHAPTER TWO

Supporting Each Other

Sober agnostics claim their place in AA

CHAPTER THREE

One Among Many

AA is a "we" program

CHAPTER FOUR

Group Life

Participation in service is a key component of sobriety for many members

CHAPTER FIVE

One Big Tent

In AA, we are one

WELCOME

"Newcomers are approaching AA at the rate often of thousands yearly. They represent almost every belief and attitude imaginable. We have atheists and agnostics. We have people of nearly every race, culture and religion. In AA we are supposed to be bound together in the kinship of a common suffering. Consequently, the full individual liberty to practice any creed or principle or therapy whatever should be a first consideration for us all. Let us not, therefore, pressure anyone with our individual or even our collective views. Let us instead accord each other the respect and love that is due to every human being as he tries to make his way toward the light. Let us always try to be inclusive rather than exclusive; let us remember that each alcoholic among us is a member of AA, so long as he or she so declares."

—Bill W., Grapevine, July 1965

The stories in this book, originally published in Grapevine, represent the shared experience of AA members who are atheists, agnostics, freethinkers or nonbelievers, who have struggled with alcoholism, yet ultimately found a common solution in AA.

Pushed to the edge of desperation by their inability to stop drinking, each finally has taken the plunge into AA—often as a last resort. Their entries into the program weren't always graceful, as a number of the stories in this volume can attest. Yet once arrived, they generally found a warm welcome—something unexpected after years of drinking and despair.

As each came to know more about AA and its spiritual program of recovery, deep reservations surfaced, with a sense that the Fellowship might not be for them.

Chapter One explores some of these reservations and how members worked through them to keep the focus on sobriety—recognizing that without sobriety all would be lost. In the book's first story, the writer of "The Transformation" asks a pivotal question often considered by many atheists and agnostics in AA: "Was a spiritual awakening necessary for lifelong sobriety? If I didn't have one, was I going to drink again?" The experience shared in this chapter puts that notion to rest, as nonbelievers of varying experience share how they are able to work the program successfully, one day at a time, as reflected in the words of Bill M. in "Sober With No God": "I know firsthand that the program of action outlined in our textbook can be effectively taken even without a belief in a god."

Secular AA members have been a part of the Fellowship since its earliest days, making significant contributions to the development of the AA program, helping to swing the doors of AA ever-wider for the steady stream of newcomers looking to AA for help. Recognizing the amazing flexibility and inclusivity of the program, in Chapter Two Carmen C. shares that "Religious and agnostic alike love Alcoholics Anonymous. It is proof that the program is spiritual and not a religion—and it does not interfere with religious or agnostic beliefs. It just lets us recover from alcoholism's misery and be well."

Still, some atheists, agnostics and nonbelievers can feel like outsiders. "It's unpopular to be an atheist," writes C.C. in Chapter Three's story "Closet Atheist," "and not every atheist admits it openly. So let's not run the agnostic or the rationalist off, back to the world of drinking."

Working together within an AA group provides the solution for many alcoholics—whatever their beliefs—leading the way to sobriety. "I've met opposition for my beliefs," writes Cara A. in the story "My Search" in Chapter Four. "I've also had people have the utmost gratitude to know they're not alone and that we can stay sober regardless of what we believe or don't believe. I've sponsored Buddhists, Christians, agnostics and those who are in the process of discovering. ... For me, the beauty of sobriety is that I can learn from everyone and anyone."

Chapter Five focuses on the many elements of AA that hold us together in unity. "As I went through the Steps, I came to believe in a higher purpose, not a higher being," writes Alex M. in "God On Every Page." "My higher purpose is to live by the principles of the Steps. The power I draw on is that unsuspected inner resource which makes me willing on a daily basis to strive for honesty, integrity, compassion, tolerance, humility, love and service." These are the hallmarks of sobriety, available to each of us in AA as we recognize our common suffering and pursue, ever more fully, our common solution.

CHAPTER ONE

Staying Sober—No Matter What

Atheists share how they work the program, one day at a time

For those who are willing—or desperate enough—to walk it, the program of Alcoholics Anonymous provides a proven pathway to recovery. Yet there is no "one size fits all" way of working the program. As the stories from atheist members in the following chapter illustrate, each AA is free to find his or her own way of staying sober.

In "Sober With No God," Bill M. writes about the hope he felt at his first meeting, hope that turned to skepticism, however, when he read "Higher Power" and "God" in the Twelve Steps. "This was clearly religion in disguise," he writes. "Still, something powerful was happening to me."

That "something powerful" was recovery and it can be had by anyone in AA, whatever their beliefs. "As an atheist, I had reservations about joining AA," says Tom F. in "Ready to Bolt." Yet, armed with the gift of desperation after a number of relapses, he realized that his fellow drunks had the answer to the dilemma of how to stay sober.

Wondering if a spiritual awakening was a prerequisite for gaining and maintaining her sobriety, Judith N. writes of her own "awakening" in "The Transformation": "It was when I took the first new woman to a meeting and when I went to the jail on Saturday morning instead of sleeping in. A spiritual awakening happened as I left the dinner table in a rainstorm to go on a Twelfth Step call and again when I said, 'Yes, I'll be your sponsor and we'll go through the book together.'"

Writes June L. in "How an Atheist Works the Steps," "I have found through my own experiences and observations of others that it doesn't matter what I believe, it's what I do that counts."

The Transformation
October 2004

"When did you have your spiritual awakening?" a woman asked me at the end of an afternoon meeting in another town. "I'm eight months sober and I don't think I'm ever going to get it."

I had been immersed in the Fellowship for four years and I didn't have an answer. An avowed atheist, I mumbled something cute like, "You'll have to ask someone older than I!" That seemed to give her hope, but it was I who was unsettled by my own evasive answer.

Was a spiritual awakening necessary for lifelong sobriety? If I didn't have one, was I going to drink again? I thought of all the stuff I was involved in—sponsoring a new woman, editing an AA newsletter, going to the jail meeting every Saturday morning, and being the GSR for my home group. Was I just whistling in the dark until the inevitable occurred? My neat little home filled with teenagers who were just beginning to trust their sober mother—were they all at risk if some manifestation of a God didn't happen to me? Was this empathy for other drunks and tolerance for the world in general all part of my mind's big con job to lull me into false security? As our AA carload headed home that night, happy and noisy and loving life without booze, I felt restless.

Among the books we had in the car was *As Bill Sees It*. I checked, and found 16 references under the "Spiritual Awakening" heading, and another 21 listed under "Spiritual Living." I determined to read them all if I had to, in order to find an answer to my question.

The first reading was Bill's account of his white light experience. I gritted my teeth and quickly went on to the second. It seemed to indicate that awakening was an ongoing thing. Could it be? The next one told me that the spiritually awakened person was in a very real sense transformed. I got excited, for if ever a drunk was transformed— from barroom brawler to PTA mother, from people-hater to lover of drunks—it was I.

The fourth entry is forever imprinted in my sober memory. It told the story of a guy who shared his life freely with others, and then said he didn't have the "spiritual angle" yet. It said it was apparent to everyone else present that he had "received a great gift, and that this gift was all out of proportion to anything that may be expected from simple AA participation," and that the rest of the group felt he was reeking with spirituality. He just didn't know it yet!

I didn't have to read on. I now knew about my own spiritual awakening. It was when I took the first new woman to a meeting and when I went to the jail on Saturday morning instead of sleeping in. A spiritual awakening happened as I left the dinner table in a rainstorm to go on a Twelfth Step call and again when I said, "Yes, I'll be your sponsor and we'll go through the book together." It began when immeasurable grace was bestowed on me, and continued as I realized that I could never repay what was given to me by the Fellowship.

A spiritual awakening was happening at that very moment as I sat in the car, letting tears of joy run down my cheeks, unashamed in front of my AA peers. I was certain that untold awakenings were in store for me as I trudged AA's road of Happy Destiny. It's been 30 years since then, and I was oh, so right.

Judith N.
Marysville, Washington

Sober for 30 Years
May 1968

As noted in my story, "The Vicious Cycle," in the Big Book, I came into the Fellowship in New York in January, 1938. At that time it was just leaving the Oxford Group. There was one closed discussion meeting a week, at Bill's home in Brooklyn—attendance six or eight men, with only three members who had been sober more than one year: Bill, Hank, and Fritz. This is about all that had been accomplished in the four years with the New York Oxford Group.

During those early meetings at Bill's, they were flying blind, with no creed or procedure to guide them, though they did use quite a few of the Oxford sayings and the Oxford Absolutes. Since both Bill and Dr. Bob had had almost-overnight religious experiences, it was taken for granted that all who followed their way would have the same sort of experience. So the early meetings were quite religious, in both New York and Akron. There was always a Bible on hand, and the concept of God was all biblical.

Into this fairly peaceful picture came I, their first self-proclaimed atheist, completely against all religions and conventions. I was the captain of my own ship. (The only trouble was, my ship was completely disabled and rudderless.) So naturally I started fighting nearly all the things Bill and the others stood for, especially religion, the "God bit." But I did want to stay sober, and I did love the understanding Fellowship. So I became quite a problem to that early group, with my constant haranguing against all the spiritual angles.

All of a sudden, the group became really worried. Here I had stayed sober five whole months while fighting everything the others stood for. I was now number four in "seniority." I found out later they had a prayer meeting on "what to do with Jim. "The consensus seemed to have been that they hoped I would either leave town or get drunk.

That prayer must have been right on target, for I was suddenly taken drunk on a sales trip. This became the shock and the bottom I needed. At this time I was selling auto polish to jobbers for a company that Bill and Hank were sponsoring, and I was doing pretty well, too. But despite this, I was tired and completely isolated there in Boston. My fellow alcoholics really put the pressure on as I sobered up after four days of no relief, and for the first time I admitted I couldn't stay sober alone. My closed mind opened a bit. Those folks back in New York, the folks who believed, had stayed sober. And I hadn't. Since this episode I don't think I have ever argued with anyone else's beliefs. Who am I to say?

I finally crawled back to New York and was soon back in the fold. About this time, Bill and Hank were just beginning to write the AA Big Book. I do feel sure my experience was not in vain, for "God" was broadened to cover all types and creeds: "God as we understood Him."

I feel my spiritual growth over these past 30 years has been very gradual and steady. I have no desire to "graduate" from AA. I try to keep my memories green by staying active in AA—a couple of meetings weekly.

For the new agnostic or atheist just coming in, I will try to give very briefly my milestones in recovery:

1. The first power I found greater than myself was John Barleycorn.
2. The AA Fellowship became my higher power for the first two years.
3. Gradually, I came to believe that God and Good were synonymous and were to be found in all of us.
4. And I found that by meditating and trying to tune in on my better self for guidance and answers, I became more comfortable and steady.

J. B.
San Diego, California

One Dark Night
February 2013

I am a sober atheist with 25 years of sobriety. I have a Higher Power. What I lack is a definition.

I found the AA program in the treatment center I attended. My trouble with "God as we understood Him" was that I understood him not to exist. But two weeks into treatment I had an atheist spiritual experience.

On the night of June 19, 1986, I was sitting in my room looking through the south window across the lake at a full moon. I found myself on my knees, realizing that the moon could be a white hole in a black curtain just as easily as a white object in an empty sky, and it really didn't matter which. Being and nonbeing were the same.

At that moment an overwhelming feeling of peace came over me. I can get that feeling back any time I want, just by remembering the experience. I stopped fighting the God question. I turned my life over to the program even though I lacked a philosophy about my Higher Power. The problem was never God's existence; it was always my own ego.

Maybe I am wrong about God. The thing is, I don't have to be right. If there is no God, the program works anyway. If there is, he must not be prejudiced against atheists. What I believe doesn't matter; what I do is what counts. I didn't get sober taking AA's inventory, but my own.

After my sudden reversal of attitude, I started taking orders without trying to make sense out of them first. I had turned over my life to something, I knew not what, and I followed the treatment center's orders from then on. It included doing the first five Steps and making a commitment to do the other seven.

When I left the treatment center they said to go to AA. I was still following orders, so I did. I returned to my day job—teaching philosophy—still without knowing what my Higher Power was or why the program works. I have learned a lot about the program during the last 25 years, but I still don't have a definition for my Higher Power. It isn't God—that's not for me—but whatever it is, it still works. I have discovered that those who believe in God have as much difficulty turning it over to a God they do believe in as I did turning it over without one.

I know what my Higher Power isn't: It isn't a guy in the sky, or a universe-maker, or the universe itself. It isn't a judge or jury; it can't be bought with faith or bribed with words of praise; it does not cause harm to others; and it never punishes or rewards. But what it is, I don't know. I don't even have a pronoun. It is not you or I, or he, she, it, they. We are still in play.

One of these days maybe I'll figure it out. I'm a pretty good philosopher. Meanwhile I am grateful for the life I have now. I owe it to an open mind at a crucial moment in my life, a whole lot of people in AA, and an as yet undefined power that became available one dark night in a Minnesota treatment center.

Alan P.
St. Cloud, Minnesota

Mysterious Alchemy
December 1990

"Frankly, B., I don't understand alcoholism. Go to AA." Those were the words of my exasperated psychotherapist, whom I had been seeing for several years in a futile attempt to stop drinking. So miserable was I that it was a struggle just to get to his office for my weekly appointments. The only thing I knew about AA was that there was a lot of talk about God. Whatever God I had once believed in became a casualty of my scientific training. I no longer believed in a personal God. Yet what did I have to lose? I was desperate.

Leaving nothing to chance, my therapist arranged for an AA member to take me to my first meeting. As I walked into the meeting room my companion explained that AA is a spiritual, not religious, program. Yet, staring at me from the wall was a poster containing the Twelve Steps, and I noted that half of them contained certain ominous capitalized words. When the meeting ended with the Lord's Prayer, surely a religious exercise, I thought, my anxiety turned to despair. Sensing this, my companion told me that I could substitute the group for my Higher Power. Those words gave me hope that there was a way out of my misery.

So I went to meetings, listened to people, and read all the literature. But I found in the "Twelve and Twelve" the strong implication that the group-as-Higher-Power is only a temporary expedient, that in time the newcomer must embrace something above and beyond the group. I was convinced this was crossing the line into religion.

Today, after 10 years in AA, I am still of that opinion, and I still do not believe in a personal God. When meetings close with the Lord's Prayer, I stand silent. I wince when I hear the words "... that probably no human power could have relieved our alcoholism ... ." For me today, it is precisely a human power that keeps me sober. That power comes in part from all of my wonderful AA friends—certainly a power greater than myself. I sometimes say at meetings, "I don't drink because you people don't want me to."

Is the group my only Higher Power? No, there is more, for I have found something "above and beyond." Far from a vaporous deity, this "something" resides within me. It is a power to which I can "turn it over." It gives a nonbeliever like myself a meaning to prayer and meditation. Oddly, I have known this thing within me long before I came to AA. It comes from many years in my profession as a mathematician.

Whenever I am unable to solve a mathematical problem, I have found that if I set it aside until another day, the answer will often come. And it comes seemingly out of nowhere, even when I am not thinking about the problem. Insights come while I'm jogging, standing in the shower, or even enduring a long-winded monologue at an AA meeting! Of course, you don't have to be a scientist to know what I am talking about; we all have sudden bolts out of the blue. After coming into AA I discovered that I could "turn over" such things as resentments, self-pity, and personal decisions to this mysterious alchemy. I now practice a daily meditation, a time of quiet when I try to turn off all verbal chatter. At such times, answers to my problems often appear. Is this what my AA friends would call God's will for me? Or am I missing something? I've thought a lot about these questions.

Sir Thomas Brown wrote in 1635: "We carry within us the wonders we seek without us." I believe there is in each of us a creative power, a force for good, an innate genius that is unique to the human species. People like St. Francis, Mozart and Einstein are extreme examples of that creative force. As a practicing alcoholic I was too engulfed in my own ego to be aware of such a power. I now know it is there if I am willing to listen. This power lies deep in the human mind, and my belief in it is an act of faith, just as my AA friends have a more conventional faith.

Today, chemistry and biology are probing the very foundations of life, and physicists talk of a forthcoming "Theory of Everything." These advances in knowledge are among the wonders wrought by the human mind. But how the mind itself works remains a mystery. As a recovering alcoholic, I prefer it that way.

I have described my own version of spirituality. I don't argue with those who believe in God. I don't proselytize. Some may think my beliefs incomplete, only half the equation. Others may say that what I have found is no different from a belief in a God, that only my language is different. I really don't care. I am comfortable with it, it works for me, and has given me an inner peace that I would never have believed possible. I am grateful to AA for forcing me to find the spiritual meaning of the Steps. The essential ingredient for my wonderful discovery is quiet—a wordless silence. It may be that I have only rediscovered what the Psalmist knew when he wrote: "Be still and know that I am God."

Bill M.
Creston, California

What We Could Never Do
February 2001

The central fact of our lives today is the absolute certainty that our Creator has entered into our hearts and lives in a way which is indeed miraculous. He has commenced to accomplish those things for us which we could never do by ourselves.

—Alcoholics Anonymous

These words from the Big Book are awfully tough for an atheist to swallow. That so-called "central fact" about a Creator is no part of my life. And anyway, even if there were a Creator, what could he do for me that I cannot do for myself? I'm the one who has to do the Steps and make amends. I'm the one who must go to meetings and do service work. What is it that I cannot do that I need a Creator to do for me?

After some months in AA, I became frustrated when I heard people in meetings talk about God doing for them what they could not do for themselves. One woman said she is now a good, loving mother for her children. She said there was no way she could have accomplished that herself. She knew because she had tried and failed for years previously. Clearly God was accomplishing for her what she could not do by herself, she concluded.

At first, this caused me to bristle. She was skipping over something important. At some earlier time, she could not take care of her children properly. Now she could. So she concluded that something miraculous had occurred. But in fact, she had learned to take care of her children in the intervening time. She was deluding herself with false modesty, crediting God with what she was doing herself; or conversely, crediting herself, by saying that what she was doing couldn't be done except by God.

But she started me thinking. When I thought about myself, I began to see that perhaps there was something to all this. And at last came a breakthrough thought. For me, AA has been like my high school typing class. Before I took the class, I could not type—no way, no how. I could hunt and peck, but I had no inkling of the true technique of typing. In theory, it is possible that I could have taught myself how to type by reading books or watching videotapes. But in fact, I know beyond a shadow of a doubt that I could never have mustered the self-motivation to learn typing on my own.

However, in typing class, there was a teacher who cared about what I was doing. She monitored my progress on a daily basis. And there were other students in the class, so we competed to be the best at typing. We were tested and graded on our work. With all this motivation, I enthusiastically learned how to type over the course of the year. Now I can reel off pages of print effortlessly.

If I compare the time before I took that class to the present, I may be tempted to conclude that a miracle occurred. Since I couldn't do it before and now I can, clearly I am not the one doing the typing. God must be doing it for me, since I can't be doing it myself.

This conclusion is evidently ridiculous. But the example contains a grain of truth. The typing class did not do the work. It did not move my fingers on the keyboard, or put in the hours of practice necessary to learn typing. I did all that myself. Yet I could never have brought myself to do that work without the typing class. The teacher, the tests, the other students, and the report card each played a role in teaching me to type. The class did for me what I could not do for myself: It motivated me to do the work to learn to type.

AA has been a similar experience for me. I have had to do all the work myself. I have had to work the Twelve Steps; I have had to attend meetings; I have had to make coffee, secretary meetings, and serve as GSR for my home group; I have had to call my sponsor every day; and I have had to read AA literature on a daily basis. No one has done that for me. And yet I could never, I would never, have done any of this work without AA to motivate me. There was nothing magic, paranormal or supernatural about this "miraculous" experience. The other AA members, my sponsor and AA as a whole have done for me what I could not do for myself: They have motivated me and given me confidence to do the work necessary to recover from alcoholism.

The central fact of my life today is the absolute certainty that AA has entered into my heart and life in a way which is indeed exceptional. It has commenced to accomplish those things for me which I could never do by myself. AA as a whole is my Higher Power.

Gabriela R.
Seattle, Washington

Sober With No God
October 2016

s an AA member who is a nonbeliever, i.e., one who does not have a god in his life, I'm grateful to be continuously sober for 26 years since my introduction to AA at the age of 53.

At my first meeting, I became hopeful that I could stay sober because inspiring, healthy and happy people shared about their drinking and their recoveries. That hope turned to skepticism, however, when I read "Higher Power" and "God" in the Twelve Steps, and then to downright dismay when the Lord's Prayer was used at the end of the meeting. This was clearly religion in disguise, a rigid way of belief, I thought. Still, something powerful was happening to me; perhaps hope was coming my way after all. I was determined to have sobriety in AA without being false to myself. I persevered despite the admonitions in our literature of the necessity of believing in a god and the belittling of my nonbelief in the Twelve Steps and Twelve Traditions.

Early on in my sobriety, I read "The Doctor's Opinion" in the Big Book, as well as modern descriptions of the disease of alcoholism in other books. They provided logical explanations of what was wrong with me and helped me to come to terms with my alcoholism. I also read widely about treatments for alcoholism and became encouraged about my chances of staying sober in AA if I "got involved in AA as much as I had drunk," for my drinking had become almost all day, every day.

I found the original six Steps in some of our literature and some letters that our cofounder Bill W. wrote. They did not have a predominance of God in them and I was able to do the Steps. They required that I give up on any notion of control over alcohol, that I take inventory, confess faults to another, make amends to those harmed, carry the message and find the willingness to take these actions. Whenever I read our textbook, *Alcoholics Anonymous*, I substitute (in my mind) AA for God or Him, or I substitute a proper noun such as Creative Intelligence. With these substitutions, the writing makes sense to me. One might say that my Higher Power is AA. I tend to say it's the love and grace that exists in AA for the newcomer.

I eventually did the suggested Twelve Steps, so that I could teach them to others. For the Third Step, which involves a prayer, I analyzed the meaning of the words and found that I could move on to the rest of the Steps to achieve the purpose stated in the prayer. The same goes for the Seventh Step. I can do the three actions mentioned in the Eleventh Step of our textbook without praying: At the start of each new day, I look to see what I can do for others; during the day I pause when confused or agitated and restart the day if necessary; and at the end of the day I constructively review my actions of that day.

Over the years, some of my AA friends have come to describe me as a Big Book atheist, and there's one who calls me "the most spiritual, open and well-read atheist I've ever met." I don't argue with anyone about belief or nonbelief. I know firsthand that the program of action outlined in our textbook can be effectively taken even without a belief in a god. That's what I say when I tell my story: I do not have a god and do not pray. I say I can be in good spirits without taking spirits.

I do use a wide range of spiritual readings (including many of the books that Dr. Bob had on his bookshelf) as inspiration to examine my life, to act morally and to love others by serving them with patience, kindness, generosity, humility, courtesy, unselfishness and tolerance. I practice these principles in AA by having a sponsor, going to meetings almost daily, attending a Big Book meeting once a week, taking the Steps and being an active member of a home group. I take to heart Ebby's imperative admonition to our cofounder Bill that we can "perfect and enlarge" our "spiritual life through work and self-sacrifice for others."

I'm involved in sponsoring men, going into jails and prisons for AA meetings, going into hospital detoxes and rehabs for Twelfth Step work, being on the local answering service list, having my name as a contact for some nearby rehabs, corresponding with and sponsoring inmates through Corrections Correspondence and carrying the AA message wherever I go around the world. I've served as GSR for my home group and DCM for my district. I was once the spiritual speaker at our area convention.

Until my retirement in 1998, I continued to teach and changed 180 degrees in my approach. In my final years of drinking, the classroom had been a stage where I displayed my knowledge. During sobriety, my focus gradually changed from what I knew to concern for what the students did not know. I once attributed booze as the source of the creativity I demonstrated in my professional work. To my surprise and delight, I found that in sobriety I developed a source of creativity that was spontaneous and intuitive rather than forced.

I'm fortunate that my family stuck by me. I have grandchildren who have never seen me drunk and know me as a loving and kind grandpa. I have students who are grateful for my teaching. I have a host of friends both in AA and in community service work. I believe that I have all of these things as a result of being an active AA member. My AA life is a testament that it's possible to be an active AA member who is sober with no god.

Bill M.
Ithaca, New York

Ready to Bolt
March 2015

As a child, I was curious about religion. Since my dad was an atheist he didn't want his children attending church. While he was adamant about his feelings, he did not ban us from going to services. However, my dad demanded equal time, so when I crept back home from Sunday services, he would ask me about the nature of the sermon I had just heard in church. Then he'd lecture me against the religion I was interested in. At that phase of my life, I considered my dad's lectures a bunch of bull. Later, while attending theology classes in college, I learned that my barely educated father was more learned than I thought. As far as I was concerned, my study of religion was over. I decided I too was an atheist.

As an atheist, I had reservations about joining AA. From the bits and pieces of information I had, I thought that AA was a religious program. Even though I wanted to be sober, I felt that I could not sacrifice my beliefs for the sake of sobriety. It seemed too big of an emotional expense, so I decided I had to do it alone.

Since I was somewhat successful at not drinking, I kept plugging away at sobriety—relapse after relapse. Sometimes I'd stay sober for a year or two and then I'd slip and drink for a while, until a drunken incident convinced me that I was out of control. Once more, I would white-knuckle it until I lost my grip on sanity. I'd rationalize that my behavior was too austere; I had to chill out. I'd make plans to drink like a normal person. It would work for a while; then my resolve would weaken and I'd go out again on a binge. Usually an incident would bring me back to reality.

One night, while driving home with one eye closed, I was wondering when this farce would end. A red light from a police car answered that question. This was my first DUI. Once again I had an incentive to quit drinking. As I aimed my pickup to the roadside, I decided I'd never have another drink. I didn't know how I would accomplish the assignment, but I knew I would go to any length to do it.

The next morning, instead of trying to keep my arrest a secret, I telephoned my ex-wife, my children and my sisters. Since they live in different communities, it was unlikely they'd have learned of my arrest. I felt that the humiliation of being truthful would reinforce my commitment to sobriety. And since I figured I'd be mandated to attend AA, I thought I should start going to meetings before I was ordered to.

As I entered the room for my first AA meeting, I was scared. I knew that this was a fork in the road. More than likely, I thought, this decision would change my life forever. Little did I know how much. I took the seat nearest to the door. I was ready to exit at the first mention of God. It didn't take long. As someone read the Preamble and the Traditions, God was mentioned over and over again. I was on the verge of bolting when I noticed the Third Tradition on the wall. I certainly had the desire to quit drinking; that meant that I had a right to stay there. So I did.

At first, I was so busy reacting to the word God that I didn't hear all the words being said. After a while, I learned that when some of the people said the word God they weren't referring to a divine entity. They were referring to a "Group of Drunks," the "Great Outdoors" or the "Gift of Desperation." That was when I started to calm down. From that moment on, I started to hear and appreciate the messages. I realized that there is a place in this program for a person with my beliefs. I just had to stop fighting and accept everything for its own value. I had to respect other people's choices. And I had a choice of making whatever was said part of my program or not. Since I identified with most drunkalogs, it wasn't hard for me to choose a group of drunks as my Higher Power. As I started to understand, I realized that my fellow drunks had the answer to my dilemma of how to stay sober. They reinforced my commitment and advised me of alternative behaviors. Like my successful predecessors, I just had to work the Steps, get a sponsor and do service.

Yes, it wasn't always so simple, but each day I learned more and made some progress. Sometimes I had setbacks, but they also seemed to strengthen my program. Joining AA was not the easiest thing I've ever done, but I've never felt so comfortable being sober before. Thanks AA.

Tom F.
Fort Bragg, California

How an Atheist Works the Steps
March 2003

My life was in shambles, and I was desperate. Following a third botched suicide attempt, I was threatened with commitment to a mental hospital. Or I could call AA. I chose AA. But I was skeptical that it was the answer because I thought I was just crazy. I thought using alcohol and drugs was a result of my problems, not a cause. I also knew that AA's program relies on a belief system that I didn't have. I told the woman who picked me up for my first meeting of my concerns. She assured me that there would be a place in AA for a crazed heathen like me.

Encouraged by the sense of relief and the lessening of fear that I felt at that first meeting, I decided right then not to struggle over God stuff. I figured if there is a God, I'd lose the battle; if there is none, it would be pointless, wasted effort. That was just under 32 years ago, and I have been sober and an active member of AA ever since. That means I have always gone to meetings (mainstream ones—no special meetings for atheist/agnostic members); I have relied on many close and trusted friends in the Fellowship; I do group service; and I try to carry the message to other alcoholics.

Despite my lack of God-understanding, which continues to this day, the Fellowship of AA has been an effective way for me to stay sober. Sober AA members have the experience of recovery, and they listen sympathetically and critically, providing advice and guidance. Their example helps me learn how to live without having to drink—ever, if I don't want to. I have found through my own experiences and observation of others that it doesn't matter what I believe, it's what I do that counts. AA provides the basis for learning what to do.

At the first meeting, I was told the obvious: not drinking is an absolute requirement for sobriety. I didn't drink, and I did whatever was necessary to avoid drinking. That required going to many meetings and reading AA books and other self-help guides. It meant accepting that people would talk about God. It meant breaking off some ill-advised associations and developing a circle of friends I could call on when I felt shaky. It meant getting involved as secretary or other group servant. It meant being willing to lie awake, or be fearful, or feel anxious, or be lonely at times. Life wasn't always easy: I suffered from depression for a time and had to concentrate on "One Day at a Time." Nevertheless, I lost my desire to drink and actually felt good about abstaining.

After I dried out and could begin to understand my condition, I wanted wellness. I wanted to live as a better person in harmony with others and with my circumstances, to be free of the chaos and conflict that had riddled my drinking life. I was told I probably needed to change every aspect of how I acted and reacted and that the AA Steps and program could help me. But what about those God Steps?

Someone once pointed out that the Steps could be considered either a description of changes that occur in recovery or a road map for making those changes. So I decided not to worry about whether I was taking the right route; instead, I focused on changing my behavior. I didn't try to force my beliefs to fit someone else's Step Three or concentrate on doing Steps Four and Five the "Twelve and Twelve" way. I simply listened to what others said about handling life events and tried what they had done in various situations. I haven't thought of my efforts as "doing the Steps," and yet I see that what I try to do approximates the direction of recovery described in the fifth chapter of *Alcoholics Anonymous*.

Besides not drinking, the most important habit I have tried to develop is not fighting circumstances. I try to accept reality instead of trying to control it. When I make that adjustment, the struggle ends and I find the freedom of knowing there is nothing more I can or must do. That sense of freedom came first when I recognized and accepted my powerlessness over alcohol (Step One). It is available in all life's adventures, if I fit myself to the flow of life (Step Three).

I remind myself regularly to trust the inner resource of the well person inside and the outer resource of the group. The track record of others and my own history show me that I can get through whatever comes, if I am patient and do what makes sense on a daily basis. This fills the intent of Step Two for me and also provides the benefits of Step Three.

I take responsibility for my actions and feelings. I think this is what Steps Four and Ten are all about—knowing and admitting my part in all my interactions and not making excuses for myself.

Consulting with others before acting on important issues and discussing past actions that bring me discomfort are integral to my life now. I am not experienced enough or objective enough to evaluate past, present, or future without a sounding board. This habit keeps my life running more smoothly and is pretty close to what Step Five describes.

I have made a great effort to stop doing those things that make me feel guilty or that diminish my opinion of myself. The burden of guilt—or fear of being found out—might lead me to seek solace in drinking. I try to do no harm and let others live their own lives. I have enough to take care of without making it worse or taking on the troubles or successes of others. This is what Steps Six and Seven contribute to recovery.

Partly to alleviate the guilt I have felt for my past indiscretions and partly because it is the right thing to do, I try to make up for wrongs through restitution, apology, or just being a better person than I was when I drank. Some are old transgressions and some are not retractable, but I do the best I can. I hope this is what Steps Eight, Nine and Ten ask of me.

In general, I like to be a do-gooder, so I help when and whom I can. This improves my relationships with my community of humans, and it makes me feel good. When I encourage another alcoholic who wants to follow the AA program but doesn't have a clear understanding of higher power, then I am doing Step Twelve.

What is missing? Step Eleven. I have no conscious contact with God—it's just not there and this does not disturb me. I try regularly to train my brain to a more spiritual viewpoint by a practice that includes contemplation, introspection, and affirmation of gratitude to have been embraced by AA. As a result, I rarely am troubled by that pervasive feeling of separation I used to feel; it has been replaced by a sense of the connectedness of all of us to one another.

Even though I didn't plan it, and even though I don't think about it as "working the Steps," Steps happen in my life as part of an AA-guided recovery. Not one of these practices involves God or believing in God, but all of them together, or each of them alone, fits the intent of the Steps. Atheism and AA's principles are not mutually exclusive, and if anyone tells you that you have to believe in God to stay sober or to remain in AA, he or she is dead wrong. I always tell nonbelievers who ask how they can do those God Steps to look for the goal of the Step and do whatever they can to meet its intent. And don't drink, no matter what happens. Nothing improves if you drink.

June L.
El Granada, California

Ceased Fighting
October 2016

The Second Step was vital in my spiritual journey. I've been hearing a lot about it recently and am pleased to find I'm not as unique as I thought. I am an atheist and not on my way to belief. The Big Book says "God is everything or else He is nothing." I chose the latter and got on with working the program.

I worked Step One prior to getting a sponsor and went back over it when I found one. Her first question was, "How do you feel about alcoholism as a disease?" I answered, "It could not be anything except a disease." We moved on, reading every word of the Big Book and talking about recovery and actions. We talked about Step Two and about AA. She was satisfied that I had found a power greater than myself using Alcoholics Anonymous.

I knew almost at once that AA could restore me to sanity. Look at all of the examples of it! I mean, I did not believe in any kind of god and yet there you all were: happier than any group of people I had ever met, and obviously no longer slaves to alcohol. You must have the answer somewhere. I was told that if I wanted what you had, I needed to do what you did. Maybe not having an intervening HP made me listen more closely or gave me more willingness to act.

In Chapter Three are the words that gave me release from the obsession to drink: "We had to fully concede to our innermost selves that we were alcoholics." I had a disease and AA was a solution that was helping countless alcoholics live a normal, sane life.

The Ninth Step Promises have come true for me: I began to know "a new freedom and a new happiness ... intuitively know how to handle situations which used to baffle us." I began to believe that my darkest day would be an asset to help another woman find a way to live comfortably in her own skin without alcohol.

Once a person online made a comment about how I was pretty high-minded to think I was doing it by myself. Being pretty new myself, I flew back a response I won't repeat here. My sponsor flinched when I told her about my retaliation. She said I had to cease fighting everyone and everything, like it says in the Big Book. She also showed me that the book also says, "Love and tolerance of others is our code." Be it a secret code or a code written as law, I knew I had to love.

My sponsor is a treasure. She is a school art teacher, which may explain her patience. But the truth is, I don't think she ever set herself up with any expectation that I would change my thinking. When I got to Step Five, I asked her, "How do I admit to 'god'?" She told me she would handle that part for me. Again, it was back to the business of the program. I came here to get sober and I got a lot more than I expected to get, and I did it without having to compromise my belief system. Our founders were truly inspired.

Paige B.
Cedar Rapids, Iowa

CHAPTER TWO

Supporting Each Other

Sober agnostics claim their place in AA

Our literature indicates that all are welcome in AA. As it says in the "Twelve and Twelve," "Alcoholics Anonymous does not demand that you believe anything." Paradoxically, there is an awful lot of talk about God.

In the first story in this chapter, "Still Agnostic After All These Years," Ann M. notes that when anyone talked in meetings about their relationship with God, "my internal switch immediately went to 'off.' ... I didn't feel at home in AA for a long time." Nevertheless, she writes, "Now, some 33 years later, I'm still an agnostic. ... Going to meetings keeps me feeling a 'part of,' as does service work. So I plan on doing what works best for me."

Later on in the chapter, Jim D. writes in "Danger, Construction Ahead" of his first sponsor, who "taught me that I don't have to drink no matter what the answers to the question of faith and Higher Power are. Whether the answer is yes, no, maybe or I don't know, I do not have to drink."

In describing her concept of a Higher Power, Carmen C. writes in "A Core of Love," "I now believe that there is a spirit in every living thing that wants it to grow and thrive. ... But if queried to describe the God of my understanding, my answer would be that I do not believe in a 'Lord' and I don't know or care if there is life after death."

Asking the question, "How have I managed to stay sober for one year being an agnostic in AA?" the anonymous writer of "I, Agnostic" answers, "I feel safe in AA because of the compassion and care. I hear stories I can relate to. I can be of service."

Still Agnostic After All These Years
April 2009

When I got sober in 1975, I had, many years before, decided that: 1) There was no God and 2) Even if there were one, he sure wouldn't want anything to do with me. So I found it very difficult in meetings when I kept getting told I had to believe in God or I would drink again. When anyone talked about his or her relationship with God, my internal switch immediately went to "off." I couldn't believe that sane, sensible humans could believe such drivel!

I endured a number of months of utter misery, saying a prayer each night that I wouldn't awaken in the morning, and crying each morning because I had awakened. (More proof that prayer didn't work, as far as I was concerned!)

I didn't feel at home in AA for a long time. If I walked into the meeting and two people were laughing across the room, I knew with a certainty that they were laughing at me. The old-timers kept telling me, "I spilled more than you ever drank—you're not a real alcoholic." (It was probably true that they spilled more than I drank!) Somehow, I kept getting asked to read the Traditions at meetings, probably because I could pronounce "autonomy" and "anonymity" without stumbling. I probably read them 20 times before I got that the Third Tradition tells me the only requirement for membership is a desire to stop drinking. I began to feel just marginally less of an outsider.

Around a year of sobriety, my first Christmas rolled around and I was at a meeting. After we had cleaned the cups, saucers and ashtrays, some of us gathered around the piano and began to sing Christmas songs. As we sang, "I'm Dreaming of a White Christmas," it dawned on me how much I was enjoying singing the song with everyone, despite my hatred of cold and snow and ice. So I realized that

I could enjoy saying a prayer with everyone without any belief in it.

At around two years of sobriety, my husband sued me for divorce. I was devastated, and out of sheer despair, started saying, "Thy will, not mine, be done," over and over. I began to feel some relief. This was my first experience that I didn't have to believe to get results from prayer. I've found that there are few limits to what you can accomplish in sobriety.

Now, some 33 years later, I'm still an agnostic. I still don't know what there is or isn't. When it says in the Third Step, "God *as we understood Him*," I know I probably will never really understand. That's OK. For me, prayer and meditation make me feel much better, and help me live a much saner, happier, more contented life. Working the Steps has been a miracle for me. Going to meetings keeps me feeling a "part of," as does service work. So I plan to keep on doing what works best for me.

Ann M.
Phoenix, Arizona

The Only Faith You Need
February 2004

I f you consider yourself an atheist or agnostic, getting sober and staying sober with the help of Alcoholics Anonymous may seem impossible, because of what I call "the God thing." But I believe it's impossible only if you let it be.

You can stay sober whether or not you believe in a Higher Power which you can or cannot define. Well-meaning members may try to refute that statement, but there is AA-approved literature to support my contention, namely page 26 of the "Twelve and Twelve," where it says "First, Alcoholics Anonymous does not demand that you believe anything."

Not quite five years ago, I was white-knuckling the railing of the landing outside my second story one-room apartment. I looked down at the pavement and decided that a nose-dive might not be decisive. I could end up severely disabled, still need that drink, and not be able to get one. I wanted to stop, but couldn't, even though I had been attending AA meetings daily for 16 months. Four days without drinking was the most I could manage on my own.

My broadcasting career was gone, my 30-year marriage was dying, and I was abjectly alone, miserable, and wanted to die. Bill, a neighbor six years sober, emerged from his apartment, said he'd heard me retching at the commode again, and suggested I go to detox one more time. I nodded in helpless agreement. Of course, I stopped to buy a pint of 100 proof vodka and drank half while driving to the detox center.

But what did I do about the "God thing," that big stone wall I pounded repeatedly with my head? I set it aside for a while. Just a while, I told myself in detox. After the grueling six-hour admission process, my shaky hands were barely able to drop 35 cents into the pay phone to call my sponsor. But it was, I guess, "the next right thing" to do.

The next day, two trusted friends from my home group surprised me with a visit in detox. They gave me a microgram of hope. Their mere presence brought to my heart what my brain had long ignored: "You are not alone. Keep comin' back. Don't quit five minutes before the miracle." Whoops, there's the God thing again, only implied, but still there in the word "miracle." Never mind, dummy, set it aside. Two more AA friends appeared at the detox center meeting that night. It wasn't their regular meeting. They were there for me. Maybe this can work for me. I would need every one of those little bits of hope.

Four days later, I checked out of detox and returned to my apartment. While climbing the 19 stairs to the landing, I opened a letter from the state unemployment office. I was not eligible for benefits, it said, because I had been fired "for cause." I leaned back against the railing and nearly fell over. The half-pint of vodka waiting under the seat of my truck began calling my name. I don't know how, but I left it there that night.

The next day, a Saturday, I drove to the clubhouse to meet my wife. After 30 years of marriage we had been separated for only 10 weeks.

She handed me my last paycheck, which had been mailed to her address, formerly my address. I wanted to know why she hadn't allowed me to visit my favorite cat for the past five or six weeks. The answer? Someone was living with her. She didn't say who, but I knew. It was a guy in the program, someone I'd picked up and driven to meetings at least a dozen times. I'd taken extra time from work to give him those rides. He wasn't one of the friends who'd visited me in detox.

The voice of the vodka in my truck grew louder. It was a night of pure hell. My mind raced from my wife and her live-in boyfriend, to the bottle, and back again—them embracing, beginning foreplay, back to the bottle, the bottle, them snuggling in front of the fireplace that once was mine, back to the bottle, the bottle, the bottle. Round and round my mind raced on that blistering hot track. Incredibly, that night my body stayed in the apartment. Finally, Sunday morning, I walked down to the truck, reached under the seat, and threw that half-filled vodka bottle, with a few more empties I found, into the dumpster. For some reason, I didn't empty the half-filled bottle. I remember thinking, Maybe it'll help some poor slob near the dump get rid of the shakes for an hour or so. Some poor slob, as if I were any different.

Unemployed and unemployable, frozen with fear of seeking even a fast-food restaurant job, I went to a lot of meetings—two, three, and four a day. I started listening. I stopped fighting the program. I lost some ego and picked up some humility. It didn't happen overnight. I still grimaced when I heard, "God did this for me and God did that, etc." but I began to take more notice of other phrases:

"The program of AA is us, supporting each other no matter what."

"Go to meetings and don't drink between meetings; sometimes it's that simple."

"Let it happen."

I didn't always fully understand what I heard. For me, awareness often comes in small increments. But I began to pick out and hang around with winners, people who, in private, gently kidded me about my nonbeliefs, but who also spoke from the heart and were very inclusive when they shared during a meeting.

"I'm no better or worse than anyone in this room" said an AA member one day, a friend who was an architect. When he said it, there might have been someone in the room who lived under a bridge or was fresh out of jail. But I know he spoke from the heart. The true democracy of his declaration was, and is, very appealing to me. But in my experience, as soon as you think you're making progress, a new challenge looks you in the eye.

A few days after I nodded approvingly at my architect friend and his appealing words, my spouse and her boyfriend appeared at a new meeting I was checking out. She and I were still legally married. She's not an alcoholic and it was a closed meeting. She never went to a meeting with me; what's he trying to do? Was he no worse than me? I asked myself. "Keep coming back" said my friends when I expressed how I truly felt. More meetings gave me a few more phrases to embrace:

"It's not important for me to think or feel right now. It is important for me to act. My actions can change how I think and feel."

"We will love you until you love yourself."

"Fake it till you make it."

For many days and through the long, slow hours of many nights that was all I could manage; I faked it. Today, nearly five years later, I hang with a bunch of winners. Some of us even play poker regularly and howl with laughter while doing the guy thing. Most of my friends are AA members who possess a quiet dignity, no matter how great the pain life lays upon them. Many seem to possess a steadfast faith in a Higher Power that most of them do call God, but when they share at meetings it's mostly kind, appropriate, and helpful—even to agnostics like me. For many long months, they loved me when I could not love myself. Now I love life and them and the newcomers.

No, I haven't "come to believe," as is strongly suggested will happen in numerous passages of the Big Book. But I can at least laugh at who and what I am. I sometimes joke about myself: "I'm so agnostic I even doubt my doubts about God." I cling to the Third Tradition and when someone attempts to inject religion into a meeting, I gently remind them, "The only requirement for A.A. membership is a desire to stop drinking."

In AA literature, I've discovered other useful phrases as well, such as "Why did we dare say ... that we must never compel anyone to pay anything, believe anything, or conform to anything?" Because to take away any alcoholic's chance of recovery "was sometimes to pronounce his death sentence."

OK, sometimes I'm not very gentle with my reminders. There is much more for me to learn, and I get lessons when I least expect it.

For an agnostic like me, getting sober and staying sober can be torturous. It can seem like my essence is being shredded and flung to the far reaches of the cosmos, leaving only a gaping hole where my soul, if I have one, used to be. But if you're an agnostic or an atheist, even with the "God thing" looming before you, give it a try. The only faith you need is faith in the AA program. Let it happen.

Michael B.
Atlanta, Georgia

Danger, Construction Ahead
March 2015

Chapter Four of the Big Book speaks directly to me with its title "We Agnostics," because I am one. I do not have a traditional religious belief in God. However, I don't disbelieve in God. I simply don't know about God. I leave disbelief to the atheist.

This lack of belief slowed me down during Steps Two and Three, but it had no impact on me staying sober during the three years it took me to get to Step Four—thanks to my first sponsor, Frank O'B.

When I read in Step Two that I should come to believe in a power greater than myself, and then read in Step Three that I should turn my will and life over to this thing called God, my busy alcoholic mind started constructing a philosophy and theology to do this. That was certainly a difficult task for an agnostic!

But Frank simply chuckled at my efforts and kept me focused on Step One. He kept saying to not drink today no matter what. He predicted that I'd never solve the mysteries of the existence of a Higher Power, the nature of God, or any of the other "deep" conundrums I was dredging up. He just kept telling me that I didn't have to drink, no matter what the answers to these weighty questions were.

He gave me a few simple guidelines: 1) He said Step Two asked me to find a power greater than myself. It did not require me to find the greatest power in the universe. Whiskey was a power greater than me, and that got me here. The rooms of AA were a greater power, and they could keep me sober. 2) Step Three did not require me to work out a total theology, just to have enough understanding to work the rest of the Steps. He said that was how any God of my understanding would want me to live: sober.

These guidelines have been enough to keep me sober for more than 30 years now, without requiring me to have either the unshakeable faith of the atheist or the solid belief of the traditionally religious.

Frank taught me that I don't have to drink no matter what the answers to the question of faith and Higher Power are. Whether the answer is yes, no, maybe or I don't know, I do not have to drink. The Steps of AA will keep me sober. Everything else is icing on the cake.

Jim D.
Toledo, Ohio

A Core Of Love
October 2007

I'm submitting my story because I have heard some controversy surrounding the issue of religion vs. spirituality within the program. I am an agnostic who loves AA. I wasn't always an agnostic. I am a product of a very religious family. My education was provided by private religious institutions.

As a child, I simply believed what I was taught, so of course I believed in God. At about the time of puberty, I started to have doubts. I couldn't live up to the standards required to "live in the state of grace"—mostly in regard to sexual thought and conduct. So the odds were that I would spend eternity in hell after I died. I couldn't see the logic in a God who would bring us into existence only to have a fair percentage of us end up in hell. I became an atheist before I graduated from high school. I can now say, God bless those who believe and live by their religious beliefs. I could not.

When I came to AA, I was past 40 years old. I had lived my entire adult life sure in my conviction that there was no God. I liked the people in AA and they told my story when they talked about themselves so I knew I was in the right place, doing the right thing. I figured I could ignore the "God part of the program" and just do the rest. But after being "sober" for a few months and having gotten over the false euphoria of believing that all I had to do was go to meetings twice a week and not drink, I hit a crisis. I became miserable. I was full of anxiety and I couldn't sleep. After 10 days of this, I considered hospitalizing myself, but I knew they would give me drugs to put me to sleep. I desperately didn't want that to be the answer.

The people I liked and respected the most in AA seemed to want to talk a lot about God in meetings, so I did the unthinkable. I took Step Three. I pictured the little guru in the "B.C." comic strip and asked him what I should do. This is the first real prayer I ever said. The answer came back in a different "voice" than the one I usually "hear" when I'm thinking and it simply said, "Just keep doing what you've been doing." Well, for the previous 10 days I'd been going to at least one meeting a day, talking to AA people, reading the Big Book, and writing in a journal. The next Step in the Big Book was Step Four. I began Step Four and knew I was going to be OK. I was able to sleep again.

There is a Higher Power. For me, this is not a theory. I know for sure that at my core is a source of moral guidance, love, wisdom and energy that, up to the moment before I took the Third Step, I didn't know existed. It has kept me sober, pulled me through some tough times, and produced moments of indescribable joy for over 18 years. I now believe that there is a spirit in every living thing that wants it to grow and thrive, while other forces, like age, disease, injury and immorality, work toward deterioration. I call this spirit "God" when I speak at meetings. But if queried to describe the God of my understanding, my answer would be that I do not believe in a "Lord" and I don't know or care if there is life after death. To some, that would make me an agnostic. But I would add that my belief in the God of my understanding gives me a better life here on earth. I am genuinely happy for you if your religious beliefs do the same. Live and let live applies well here. Religious and agnostic alike love Alcoholics Anonymous. It is proof that the program is spiritual and not a religion—and it does not interfere with religious or agnostic beliefs. It just lets us recover from alcoholism's misery and be well.

Carmen C.
Port St. John, Florida

Spiritual Honesty
April 1985

As a recovering member of Alcoholics Anonymous and an agnostic, I would like to present a few thoughts on our Fellowship from an agnostic viewpoint.

One thing that makes my own experience unusual is that I came into the program 18 years ago professing a conventional belief in God and had no problem accepting the essential part God is believed (by the majority of AAs, past and present) to play in recovery. One of my strongest beliefs is and always has been that a successful, happy recovery is achieved through personal changes brought about by working the Twelve Steps.

After many slips, the last only two years ago, I concluded that one important area I had failed in was an unqualified commitment to honesty. One black memory of my past was a bad conduct military discharge for narcotic use, a source of such shame that I had never told anyone about it except my wife. At my next opportunity as a speaker, I included this episode, and with it went all the guilt I had carried for 30 years.

Coming honestly to terms with my agnosticism was slower and more difficult. The first part was admitting that, even though I considered myself a believer, I had really always lacked the quality of genuine and heartfelt faith. My wife and many people I admire most, both in and out of the Fellowship, have a beautiful faith, which I respect. I harmed myself in 15 years of hypocrisy in the program, proclaiming a belief I did not really hold. Today, admitting I lack faith does me no harm, because it causes me no needless concern; being different, dissenting from the views of a majority of my peers, is not a source of guilt.

The next step was a renewal of my commitment to the Twelve recovery Steps, mainly those Steps that refer directly or obliquely to God. In my first home group, so long ago, I discovered a power greater than myself; that power of love and good helps us recover through sharing, accomplishing together what we could never do alone. I am an agnostic because I cannot honestly say that I have ever experienced or felt anything I am willing to accept as proof of God. I do believe in the human soul, above and apart from our physiology and mortality, even though I cannot prove the soul exists. Some will see a contradiction here, but for me it is just another example of being different, nothing more.

The suffering newcomer to our program is looking for a lifeline, a way out of the hell alcoholism has brought him to. Those who have managed to retain their belief in God suddenly find it all beautifully reaffirmed and can have a relatively rapid transition as recovering members. Others can be turned away by being presented with religious, spiritual, or abstract concepts they are unable to accept or relate to. At their first meeting, newcomers will probably be invited to join in the Serenity Prayer or the Lord's Prayer and will hear a reading

of the Twelve Steps. In "How It Works," they will hear how we made
a decision to turn our will and our lives over to the care of God as we
understood him; how, after a searching and fearless moral inventory,
we were ready to have God remove all these defects of character and
humbly asked him to remove our shortcomings; how we sought to
improve our conscious contact with God, praying only for knowledge
of his will for us and the power to carry that out. They may also hear
the disclaimer that AA is not a religious organization, but might still
get the impression we come fairly close.

I ask that we listen for newcomers who cannot understand or accept the spiritual side of our program, that we stick to the meat-and-
potatoes approach and just ask them to try 90 meetings in 90 days
with an open mind. We may save a life, for that is what staying or
leaving means for many—life or death.

We who are different, whether newcomers or old-timers, need to
have the benefit of one of our most important slogans, "Live and Let
Live."

W. H.
West Lebanon, New York

Three Strikes, You're In!
March 2014

When I came to AA at age 21 I had to overcome not one,
not two, but three obstacles that made getting sober
more challenging than it needed to be. The first hurdle
was that I was too young. There were nothing but older folks in my
first few meetings, leaving me feeling alone and very different. The
average age in the room was more than double mine.

Second was that I was gay. I knew I had to be the only gay person
in AA for sure. Everyone was talking about his or her spouse, while I
hadn't even had a real adult relationship yet.

Finally, I considered myself to be either an agnostic or an atheist. As a result of my religious upbringing, I entered AA with feelings of worthlessness, fear of rejection and shame. Meetings often closed with the Lord's Prayer, and were filled with numerous references to God. I thought there was no way this Fellowship was going to be right for me.

But I was desperate and had nowhere else to turn. In one of those early meetings someone said, "The only requirement for membership is a desire to stop drinking." That, I surely had. My drinking was daily and around the clock. And even though I was "too young," I was consuming mass quantities of alcohol and having blackouts all the time. So even though I felt terribly unique, I needed what AA had to offer to stop drinking. So I stayed.

It's been 32 years since those early days, and it's almost embarrassing for me to admit that only in the past year have I been completely open about my identity in mainstream meetings. I feel a growing obligation to share about the hurdles that held me back in those early days of my recovery. Now I can share this for those who may struggle similarly—and for myself. My openness is the best indication of my own self-acceptance.

So dare to be as authentic as you can. Sameness is boring. I am grateful my terminal uniqueness didn't chase me away from AA. Today I celebrate the differences that made the beginning of my recovery difficult. The Fellowship made me feel like I belonged for the first time in my life. I owe a debt of gratitude to those who supported and accepted me as I am. As a result, I'm at peace with myself and life is good. Thanks to the Third Tradition.

Jack B.
Oakland, New Jersey

I, Agnostic
April 2011

I do not intend to offend those who believe in a God or have spiritual faith in a "Higher Power." I believe that most religions or faiths are good if their principles are love, compassion and comfort, encourage personal positive growth, and are not used incorrectly to harm or distress others.

As of August 1, 2010, I have been sober for one year. I am a 57-year-old white male who leans more on the atheist side of the fence, but since Chapter Four in the Big Book is titled "We Agnostics," I will refer to myself as an agnostic. Personally, I don't believe in a God or a personal "Higher Power" at the present time. I am sober today because of the Fellowship of AA, Step One and Tradition Three. AA saved my life.

A little over a year ago, I sat in a psych ward singing "Happy Birthday" to myself after trying to commit suicide in the midst of an alcohol-poisoned breakdown. This was the second time within months that I found myself in a 72-hour lockdown under similar alcohol-related events. Between those two "visits," I had gone to AA, found a sponsor and was sober for 89 days. But the fear that unless I accepted a God or a Higher Power, I would be "doomed to an alcoholic death" and face certain disaster, turned me away. It scared me enough that I couldn't get past Step One.

I was told my Higher Power could be anything: the powerful ocean waves, a beautiful tree or whatever I liked. So I started praying to the trees and faked it with my sponsor, saying I had done Steps Two and Three. Later, I moved away from the tree idea and started to believe that the sun rising outside my window was my Higher Power. The sun is certainly powerful, that much I understood. And it worked, for a while. Soon I began to feel silly asking the sun or trees or the wind for help.

My second "visit" to the ward followed and I wound up in lockdown. To this day, I remember vividly the images of the locked door, the psychiatric doctor's face and hearing his words very clearly: "If we ever see you in here again, you will be going away for a very, very long time!" Those images and those words frightened me sober. After 10 years of alcoholic insanity, I got it. It was up to me to find a solution.

During those 10 years, and up to that day, nothing had convinced me I had a problem. The numerous visits to hospital emergency rooms, my personal doctor telling me that if I continued to drink (four to six bottles of red wine, plus four to six small bottles of vodka a day) I was going to die of liver disease in a couple of years, flying to another country so I could drink and not be recognized, (in Australia they have pubs that are open 24/7!), submitting myself to some degrading and depraved human activity, allowing my career to sink and hurting many on the way, swallowing a bottle of sleeping pills, sitting in a warm bath with my neighbor's Stanley knife I had borrowed (he doesn't want it back) and my body consistently raging with enough alcohol to kill a horse. Nothing woke me up until that day in the psych ward. For me, it was a very clear message. I was powerless over alcohol and my life was in ruins. I needed help, big time.

How have I managed to stay sober for one year being an agnostic in AA? First, I walked back into an early morning AA meeting, and was welcomed back. Second, I read Step One again: "We admitted we were powerless over alcohol—that our lives had become unmanageable." That was me.

This Step is the simplest, yet the most important in my life. I was completely powerless over alcohol. It controlled my life, my very being, poisoning my body and mind. My life had become unmanageable and I was tired of running away. Eventually I had nowhere to run.

Third, I read Tradition Three (probably for the first time): "The only requirement for A.A. membership is a desire to stop drinking." That's it? I'm in.

I am an alcoholic. I have the disease, I'm aware of it and doing my best, day by day, to keep it arrested with the help of my friends and the

Fellowship of AA. Yet I am still an agnostic. I feel safe in AA because of the compassion and care. I hear stories I can relate to. I can be of service.

The Big Book has helped millions find comfort in their own existence. I am one of those people. If the Big Book has offered comfort, should we question the small percentage of it that makes us uncomfortable or do we simply accept the bigger picture, which is that AA has saved our lives?

I once asked an atheist who was 20 years sober in AA, "What about the Big Book, with all the mention of God and spiritual messages?" "There are great tools to be used within those pages," he said. "Find and use what you need in your journey of recovery. The Big Book is full of wisdom and hope."

If you are an agnostic/atheist, take what you need from the program and use the tools for your own personal journey. Do not let the occasional (over) use of the word God frighten you away. There are some great shares in meetings that everyone can relate to. And who knows? Some of us may even shift from our hardcore stance and one day find a Higher Power of our own. Remember, this is AA ... anything can happen.

One day at a time.

Anonymous

The Uncertainty Principle
September 1995

If I don't believe in a God, what is my Higher Power? How can I apply the Steps? What is it that helps me, an agnostic, get sober and stay sober? I gave up searching for an understanding of my Higher Power. Call it a character defect if you will, but I simply cannot believe. So how do I apply the principles of AA? How do I stay sober?

Strange as it may seem, I am helped mostly by Steps Three and Seven. I turn my will and my life and all things over to the care of anything but me. Instead of going against the stream of life, running my head against walls, trying to do the impossible, I turn the outcome of my endeavors to the natural flow of things. I constantly remind myself that I cannot control my fellow humans. Their lives are controlled by the laws of nature, just as mine are. I remind myself, whatever I do, that I never have all the facts affecting the outcome. I do the best I can with the data available, but I can't plan on the outcome. In physics there is something called an "uncertainty principle." Chance and the unknown play too much a part in my daily life to insist on a certain outcome.

But this "turning over" is essentially an act of nonaction. Nonaction in the past was my downfall; it led to concentrating on myself and my problems. So what else must I do? The key here lies in the recognition that the worst problem for an alcoholic is self-centeredness. The solution to that problem is concentration on others. What keeps me sober and serene is the very act of letting go of resentments, self-pity, fear of others, and whatever else keeps my thoughts going in circles about myself. While I'm occupied with paying attention to the needs of others, I'm free of myself. I don't mean to imply that I shouldn't take care of myself. My natural needs must be met. But no more is required.

Step Seven, which asks the Higher Power to relieve me from all defects that stand in the way of my usefulness to my fellows, is the active complement of Step Three. In the Seventh Step prayer I see that the believer simply asks to be a good person. A good person is a person who does no harm to others, a person who helps others. As long as I'm a good person, I need not fear others. As long as I take care to know what acts of mine might harm others, I'm not concentrated on myself, but on others. I stay sober. In Steps Four, Five and Six, I've learned what defects of mine tend to hurt others. Constant vigilance against these defects keeps me on my toes, keeps me away from getting stuck in the rut of self-pity, fear and resentment. I practice the opposite of the defect. Instead of letting fear of failure lead me into procrastination, I practice doing difficult things first. Instead of letting impatience bring my brain to a boil, I practice patience. It's easy to fall back into bad habits. By practicing the opposite, I practice and acquire good habits. Still, I need Step Ten to avoid falling back, and meditation in Step Eleven to learn more of what is required of me to stay happy and serene without a drink.

My Higher Power? The laws of nature—those I know of, and those I don't know of.

Oktavia C.
Galveston, Texas

Continental Shift
April 2010

P robably everybody in AA has heard people talking at meetings about "that Higher Power thing"—how the whole God business gave them pause, or made them think that maybe AA was not really for them. Usually these people go on to say how they've changed, and how much their Higher Power means to them now. Our AA founders clearly anticipated this issue, and included the "We Agnostics" chapter in the Big Book. This chapter doesn't work for me. And it should, because agnostic is exactly what I am.

Perhaps I should start by noting my belief that no one has greater faith than an atheist. Confidence that there simply is no God requires a level of certitude that I can only marvel at. On the other hand, certainty that there is a God also exceeds my mortal grasp. I suspect that there is a God. But suspicion falls way short of faith. "We Agnostics" says, "You may be suffering from an illness which only a spiritual experience will conquer." So says "We Agnostics"—and I can accept that. The problem is, I don't know what is not a spiritual experience.

I'm one of those people who apologizes to a weed when I yank it out of a flowerbed. Killing an insect, for me, presents a moral quandary every single time. Is that spiritual, or simply insane? I just don't know.

I see potential sins, and virtues, everywhere. But I don't know what or who God is, or whether God is. I'm not even sure that's any of my business.

More to the point, I also don't think my faith, or lack of it, is a determinant of my sobriety. Yet, it is clear from "the chapter to the agnostic" that the Big Book is talking about reformed agnostics—that maybe if I just keep coming back, the scales will fall from my eyes. What's more, the book strongly implies that if I do not shed my agnosticism, I cannot stay sober. "Humph!" say I.

Deities aside, even as an unpersuaded agnostic, my universe features no shortage of powers greater than myself. Plate tectonics and erosion spring to mind. So too, "the green fuse that drives the flower," as Dylan Thomas put it, or "the strength of spring" Bob Dylan sang about. Powers greater are all around me. And that's OK. Can mere continents grinding together keep me sober? Can erosion? Too soon to tell, I guess. But so far, I've got no complaints. Haven't had a drink all day.

In his beautiful little biography of St. Augustine, Garry Wills wrote, "We seek one mystery, God, with another mystery, ourselves." Augustine himself elected not to explain it: "Since it is God we are speaking of, you do not understand it. If you could understand it, it would not be God."

Now that's a faith I can live with.

Bert W.
Prescott, Arizona

CHAPTER THREE

One Among Many

AA is a "we" program

Often feeling left out, many secular AA members have struggled to feel at home in the Fellowship. As the stories in this chapter relate, find a home they have—as productive, sober members of the AA community, without compromising their beliefs.

As one anonymous writer puts it in the story "An Atheist Asks," "As a member of AA, I believe this is a 'we' program. 'We' have a problem." Yet that "we" goes further for the Fellowship, as the self-admitted atheist notes, "'We' can't claim to love and include everyone who wants to stop drinking—and then make that love conditional on the acceptance of spiritual beliefs."

"Spiritual growth and experiences are not limited to orthodox believers in a deity, any more than the disease of alcoholism is limited to skid-row bums," J.B. writes in "Is 'Agnostic' a Nasty Word?" Summing up, J.B. continues, "In the final analysis, the individual's achievement and continued maintenance of healthy sobriety are dependent upon his recognition of a Power greater than himself. Whether he personifies it in a deity or understands it as a dynamic force, it is nevertheless a Power for good."

In "Closet Atheist," C.C. expresses the feelings of many who at different times have felt "apart from" the Fellowship. "I think what keeps me sober more than anything else is the AA Preamble: 'Alcoholics Anonymous is a fellowship of men and women who share their experience, strength and hope with each other that they may solve their common problem ...' ... So let's have a little tolerance—tolerance perhaps of the unexpressed secret beliefs of the person next to you."

Out of the Closet
March 2015

I t's 8:35 PM on Saturday and the speaker has just suggested the topic "How God works in your life." I settle back in my seat, preparing myself to be open to receiving the message of recovery. I've become very good at listening and finding a message. It's rare that I walk away from an AA meeting without taking home a little hope.

I've been coming to this particular meeting for 10 years. In November, I celebrated 27 years of continuous sobriety in the same county, and the speaker knows this. But I won't be called on tonight; in fact, I'm rarely called on at all in Alcoholics Anonymous these days. You see, I'm an atheist. I'm not resentful of my standing in AA, at least not often. And because I strive to stay a part of AA, most of the time I feel a kinship in the rooms. But there are nights that I wonder; there are nights that I feel separate.

I came into AA one month shy of 21 and, amazingly, it stuck. This means that if I stick around these rooms and don't have a drink, in a few years I'll be 50 years old and have 30 years of recovery, never having had a legal drink of alcohol. I came to these rooms without having lost a lot because, in truth, I had not gained anything in my short life, except for an obsession to drink. When I got here I was seething with hate, rage, pain and attitude, a common combination I've come to witness over the years. These emotions were all I had except for a small voice in me that didn't want to be in pain or die, and that voice was enough to keep me coming back.

I had been raised in my parents' religious beliefs and had rejected the idea of God at an early age. I remember questioning their beliefs and the concept of God, as early as 8 years old. Actually, by the time I found my first love, alcohol, I had rebelled against the whole idea of God. Alcohol had dragged me down by the age of 12, so it's no wonder I felt hopeless by age 20.

The first years of my recovery were spent trying to live without alcohol. I worked the Steps with a sponsor and tried to follow directions. If you measure success by whether one drinks or not, then I was successful. However, I did learn some valuable lessons in the first 15 years of my recovery. I did service, worked the Steps and continued to go to meetings, but there was a deep unrest inside me. I had copied what other people had done and pretended to believe the way that they did. I learned the song and dance that was most acceptable to AAs in my community. I could parrot the Big Book and say all the things that people wanted to hear, and yet there was something missing. I wanted people to like me, to tell me I was OK, and they did for those first 15 years.

Then there was a point in my recovery when things began to change. Situations happened in my life that pulled the rug out from under me and I was forced to change my life and how I was in the world. I was forced to open my eyes, and the changes began. They were gradual and subtle at first. I started seeking, not God, but something that I could believe in, something that made sense to me. It started with returning to school and becoming interested in the world outside of AA. Now, I've heard horror stories about people who stop making AA the center of their lives. I know many people who only socialize in AA—and that's what works for them. I did not leave AA, but I took the principles that I learned in the rooms and went out into the world. I learned to listen to that healthy inner voice that we all have, if we have stayed on this path for any amount of time. I found interests and hobbies outside of the rooms and frequently pulled my friends in AA out with me to experience opera and theater. I began, for the first time in my life, to really thrive.

I came to the knowledge that I was an atheist more than five years ago, but it took some time for me to get up the nerve to step out of the closet with the general AA public. I did it while speaking at an Easter Sunday morning meeting over three years ago. At least 3 people got up and left. Truth is that I hadn't planned it that way. Simply put, I just said what I believed and felt I needed to say out loud. I had been silent in meetings for over two years prior to that Easter Sunday. I had been listening for my truth, and it finally spoke up.

I have heard it all since then. I've been told that I'm really a Buddhist, a Native American and, of course, that I will get drunk if I don't mend my ways. There are those who ignore me and those who don't understand me, yet I strive to be polite to all of them, regardless. Most important are those who don't care what I believe in because they love me and leave me to my beliefs, although we do have great conversations over coffee about our differences.

I've often been asked what I do each day to stay sober without a God. I do the same things that any believer does—minus the reliance on a God. I get up each morning and focus on what needs to be done. I strive to be the best person I can be, to carry understanding, love and tolerance in my dealings with my fellow human beings. I turn things over, not to a God, but to the knowledge that I live in a world that I cannot control. I take responsibility for what's happening in my life and endeavor to be proactive on those things that I can take action on. I'm not perfect, not by a long shot, but I'm not worse at the practicing of these principles than anyone who believes in God. I find peace in the journey of life and living in this day. I still work the Steps and yes, I don't work them with the word God in them. I have a sponsor, sponsor other women and do service. I believe strongly in doing service outside of AA as well, and believe that finding balance in all I do is the key to a strong recovery and love of life.

There have always been atheists in the history of humankind. Sometimes they have been ignored and sometimes persecuted, but they've always been present. There are atheists in AA. I have met some of us and we are productive members of AA as well as of our communities. The Big Book was written to include more than just a small slice of humanity, and there is room for us atheists. The Twelve Traditions were written to insure the openness of AA to all those who have a desire to stop drinking. I'm grateful to the program of Alcoholics Anonymous. I have found a way of life here that first answered my drinking problem and then gave me solutions to my living problems.

Anonymous

I Got Out of the God Business

January 1970

Fourteen years ago, I attended my first meeting of Alcoholics Anonymous. I was looking for freedom from fear and alcohol. The struggle has often been discouraging, but worth every minute of it. Some of the sober moments have been pure, undisguised hell, but what I had before was infinitely worse.

If I go back to drinking, at best I may only have a bad hangover. At worst, my brain may go soggy, leaving me a vegetable for life. Worth it? For one lousy drink?

I started drinking in my mid-teens, and the next nine years were fun, although my wife thought otherwise. On my 24th birthday, I partially found out what was so obvious to others—that I was a problem drinker. But I was not fully convinced, so it naturally followed that I did nothing about it. Three more hellish years went by before I found AA. At once, I had a feeling of belonging, a feeling that someone cared. The AAs had all gone the same sort of route as I had, so they understood me. I can't describe the wondrous feeling of relief that flowed over me, to know that I didn't have to drink anymore, to know that I only had to follow some simple suggestions to find freedom from both alcohol and fear. One day at a time.

It was pointed out to me that if I would change my attitude, my whole life would change. But if I held on to my old ideas and ways, I would very likely end up by getting drunk. I decided to give the program a good try.

When I came to AA, I still believed in God, or so I thought—and continued to think for another 12 years. I meant the God I used to bargain with: "Get me out of this, and I'll never do it again." Well, I soon learned that that wasn't quite cricket. Still, for the next 12 years I went along with this "God as I understood Him." But I didn't quite buy the idea, even though I gave it lip service. Do I sound as if I was mixed up? I was. I never gave my beliefs any solid, analytical thought. Now at last I have, and I know that I no longer believe in mumbo jumbo and fairy tales.

Just over two years ago, I had to go to a psychiatrist. I knew I should have done it long before, but I had been afraid. I felt that I had to be ready to see the psychiatrist before he could be effective for me. Just as in approaching AA, you do have to be ready.

One problem was that my wife was driving me around the bend, and I was letting her. I could not handle the situation, and for two ghastly years I had teetered on the edge of a drunk, knowing full well that it would be no answer. Keeping that knowledge foremost in my mind saved me. The length of my AA membership, plus many friends, undoubtedly contributed to saving my sanity. But in the end these alone were not enough. Even though my problem was not the sort of thing that I could talk about, I tried to on three occasions. The first time, I got a blank stare; the second time, I got "I've troubles of my own." Third time around, I got sympathy, which was nice, but no answer.

So for nearly a year I went to the psychiatrist. He showed me how to handle an intolerable situation: to roll with the punch, to adapt—or else. During the same period, I chanced upon a book that helped me to see my way around and out of mysticism and the God business.

If you are easily upset, don't read any further. But if you do read on, try to keep an open mind. Remember, I do not speak for AA. This is only my opinion, and I'm supposed to be entitled to that. If the God business works for you, then by all means use it. In everyday matters such as reroofing my house or growing a crop of spuds, God doesn't do the job or pay for it, nor should He, if He existed. And I do not believe that if I am killed in a car accident, "He willed it," nor that if I live to be 103 (horrible thought), "He willed it." I do not believe that if my son is born mentally or physically defective, "God willed it." Never! And my son was born defective in both areas. What's that you say? A "God of love"? I just don't buy that. It simply doesn't add up.

Science has proven that we evolved from unicellular "things" millions of years ago. Doctors have discovered many of the whys and wherefores of mental and physical deformities. There is nothing mystical about life. It is mysterious sometimes, yes. But intelligent thought and years of research have unlocked many of its secrets. As research goes onward, more secrets will be revealed.

You may wonder why or how I'm still sober, or say, "No wonder he had trouble!" You may say that without a belief in a higher power, nobody can stay sober, or at least not happily so. Rubbish!

I know a large number of people who are perfectly sincere in their belief in a Higher Power, yet are still drunk! Some of them have been in and out of AA for many years. I know one who has been in AA for 19 years and will have a 24-carat snit if you use the Lord's name in vain. Yet this same man has yet to make his first sober year.

A few weeks ago, serious consideration was given to asking a man to leave a meeting because he had stated clearly that he didn't believe in God. He said that, for him, the idea was entirely inconsistent with all the evidence he could see. Of the 25 or so people there, nine got up and walked out. There were only four or five who did not appear to be deeply offended. The rest were filled with pity for the guy, or anger against him—sometimes both. Well, so much for the open minds we are supposed to have.

It is not necessary to be bubblingly, overflowingly happy to stay sober. True, it does help if you are, but it is not necessary.

Three factors keep me sober: (1) the many people I know in AA (if they can do it, so can I, with their help); (2) the principles as laid out in our Twelve Steps; (3) me. That's right—me! If I don't thoroughly cooperate and try, then I'll sink back into the old ways. These three factors are in a constant state of change as far as their strength goes for me. Sometimes, it is number one that is strongest; other times, it is number two; at still other times, it is number three. Singly or in unison, it matters not how, they work for me.

My purpose in writing this is in the hope that I may reach the drunk who doesn't believe in "God as you understand Him." I'm finding more and more around like me, others who don't believe. I'm grateful for the courage of that one man who stood up to be counted. He sincerely believed his words needed to be said for the drunk who thinks as we do. After all, communication is the name of the game, isn't it? Those who are believers are entitled to believe as they wish, and it seems to work for countless thousands of them. The guy or gal who arrives at the same conclusion that I did is also entitled to his opinion. Please don't deny us the right to a say in print.

AA will not work for those who simply need it, only for those who truly want it. I did at the start, and still do. So that is why, 14 years later, I'm still sober. We accomplished together what I was incapable of doing alone.

And finally, it is really so very simple: Just for today, I'll not take that first drink.

R. S.
Vancouver, British Columbia

Is There Room Enough in AA?
October 1987

Recently my 28-year-old son began to recognize his growing problem with alcohol (an episode with the law helped get his attention) and went to his first AA meeting on his own behalf. As a child he had been to meetings with me, now 16 years sober in AA. Over the years he has watched the improvements in my life and I am sure he knows of AA's high success rate for alcoholism recovery. When he was about 18 and I spoke to him about the probable inheritability of alcoholism and the strong potential for him to become alcoholic he said, "Don't worry. If I find out I've got it I'll just go to AA."

The time has come for him, but his initial visit to AA for himself was a disaster. He says the only member there who approached him was a woman, well-meaning no doubt, who began telling him the first thing he had to do was find a belief in God. This woman's suggestion that God would bring about his recovery from alcoholism is about as absurd to him as a suggestion to use bloodletting or a few voodoo treatments would be to most of us in the modern Western world. You see, my son, like me, is an atheist.

When my son told me of his encounter, I tried to point out to him that I and an agnostic woman he knows have had success with AA's program. But his comment was: "Maybe you can handle that stuff but I don't want to waste my time with it. I'll just have to find some reasonable way to work this out." Like many alcoholics he may still be somewhat uncertain about whether he wants to make a commitment to sobriety. The heavy-handed religiosity he found provided exactly the excuse he needed to bolt and run. Unfortunately his assessment of AA as a group of religious fanatics was supported by two of his friends who had also sought help from AA and had rejected it for the same reasons after similar experiences.

The experience of my son and his friends led me to consider why and how I was able to find compatibility between AA's teaching and my own atheistic philosophies. My background prepared me better, I think. I had been raised in a religion—one that I rejected, but also one that I understand and do not feel any particular animosity toward. I simply do not regard belief in God as supportable by evidence, rational, nor necessary for happy living. That was true for me when I got to AA and continues into my long sobriety. I suspect that my earlier contacts with religious people whom I loved and trusted made me more tolerant or at least less suspicious of their ideas. Also the man who urged me to call AA was an atheist in AA and had forewarned me of the strong God orientation of many people. This AA member had suggested I reveal my ideas at once and ask that I be referred to someone with similar ideas.

Furthermore, I think my first call to AA was crucially different than my son's. I told the woman who came to take me to a meeting of my atheism and my concern that AA might not work for me. She respected my attitude and pointed out to me how AA, regardless of God or higher power, had a great deal to offer that was very practical. AA would (and did) provide friendly counseling from people who had followed the same path as I. In the nurture of the Fellowship I could develop living skills that I had neglected for so many years. The Fellowship would be an immediate source of social contact with those who also did not drink. AA could teach me to be a social being without having to use the drugs I was accustomed to. She told me the Twelve Steps could be liberally translated to be an excellent guideline for reasonable and harmonious living with others and with myself. Not that first night, nor in the years of our friendship since, did she tell me that I must find God in order to stay sober.

Over the years I have been reticent about my atheism at AA meetings because I know it goes against the grain of most members and is contrary to AA literature. The chapter to the agnostic is quite clear in its message that somehow all of us will eventually find God—that such belief is fundamental to humans. I do not agree, but when God or higher power is discussed at meetings I tend to pass, except at the small close-knit group I attend. Otherwise, my contributions are mostly limited to topics which address practical sobriety. I have refused requests to speak at meetings for several years because I didn't think I should speak openly of how AA works in my life.

Perhaps that was wise of me when I was still quite mad and the benefits of AA were not so obvious in my life. It seemed unacceptable to state that sobriety is possible without believing in God when my sobriety was so short-term and my mental and emotional equilibrium was so tenuous. But years have passed and all the promises of AA have come to me. My life is richer than I could have ever imagined and I owe it entirely to the AA program. You see, AA's Twelve Steps and the exchange of ideas with other recovering alcoholics are so effective in combating this disease that, for some of us, these tools alone are enough to gain a rewarding sobriety. It concerns me that many do not realize this fact.

Rarely do I hear anyone else admit to nonbelief in God, and I have held the impression that very few atheists remain in AA. The man who sent me to AA subsequently abandoned the Fellowship. Often I have wondered whether the atheists commonly go away or if they finally conform out of greater willingness or more determination to believe than I have. Recently I have come to suspect that neither is the case. I hear so little from atheists in AA because those of us who do not believe in God keep quiet about it. I have done so partly out of timidity and partly to avoid the comment that the admission of atheism frequently brings: that I will someday believe or I will get drunk.

The relationship between a belief in God and sobriety cannot be demonstrated to be consistent. Over the years I have watched many people get drunk even though they professed a belief in God and a clear understanding of him. The clergy suffer as much from alcoholism as any other group of people. Clearly a belief in God is no assurance of not returning to drinking. I am convinced from demonstrations all around me that sobriety is the result of one recovering alcoholic helping another, with both striving to achieve the orderly, responsible lives described in AA's Twelve Steps.

Often it is said in AA meetings that AA is not a religious program but a spiritual program. However, in AA most spirituality is spoken about in religious terminology. The term God (with capital "G") and references to "him" and "his will" are right out of Western Judeo-Christian writings. We cannot expect a newcomer atheist to read between the lines of religious jargon and conclude that a phrase like a "conscious contact with God" could be translated to mean "an enlightened attitude."

We all need to be able to explain to newcomers how AA works in terms that particular alcoholic can understand. Never would I seek to explain AA in my own atheistic interpretation to an alcoholic who believes in God and suggest that he would do well to modify his perception in order to get or stay sober. Instead I can speak to the person about God from the many references and explanations which abound in AA literature. Yet it is probably more difficult the other way around. A God-oriented AA member doesn't have a large supply of ideas from atheists available to share with the newcomer atheist. Too few of us state our positions in meetings; too little is written in AA's literature.

J. L.
Oakland, California

An Atheist Asks
August 2011

I am an atheist. I am also a sober member of AA, and have been for over four years.

The first AA meeting I attended, in Buffalo, New York, was one of the most unique and powerful experiences of my life. I have no interest in either promoting or condemning AA. I have seen a good number of people find help in AA. I have also seen a good many people come to AA in desperation, only to walk away frustrated that they could not find the help they needed.

As the years go by, and as I continue attending meetings regularly, I have become aware of certain prevailing attitudes which I believe do considerable harm to AA's main purpose. I feel compelled to oppose such harmful ideas and pronouncements which, I believe, stand in the way of an honest, open and healing dialogue.

I've been able to find help in AA because I was raised with an understanding of many concepts which AA takes for granted. The use of the word God, for instance. The book *Alcoholics Anonymous* goes to great lengths to appear accepting and inclusive of all who suffer from alcohol addiction. However, the book is clearly written in a moral tone, more Christian than anything, and its very language seems more welcoming to those of a Christian background. Furthermore, while every individual is promised the freedom to choose his or her own idea of a Higher Power, the frequent use, and capitalization, of the word "God" and the wording of the suggested prayers, does not seem inclusive of any non-Christian concept. There are almost no references in the AA literature to any spiritual practices, outside of Christian beliefs.

Looking into our basic text, we are assured at the beginning of the chapter titled "We Agnostics" that many of our Fellowship's founding members were either atheist or agnostic, but the chapter crescendos in a coercive pitch that casts atheism as a flaw which must be corrected if one hopes to stay sober.

This polemic raises a very important question, one which is argued about either overtly or covertly at many AA meetings: Is our primary purpose to stay sober—or to find faith in a Higher Power?

The literature, in a very circular logic, suggests that these two issues are solved together through the taking of the Steps. This leaves the atheist or agnostic with a huge problem when he comes to the Second or Third Step. His fellows in the program may try to cheer him on the concept of a Higher Power, telling him he's totally free to choose his own idea of God. What if his choice is to believe in no God?

We may hear in the words of many well-meaning believers that we are free to choose the group, the meeting, or the "whatever" as our Higher Power. The insinuation is ever present that those who choose not to believe in God are somehow inadequate.

We hear in meetings how God is doing for our fellows what they could never do for themselves. Someone gets a job, a car, a house, or recovers from an illness—and this is somehow proof of God's involvement in their personal lives. We all know that non-Christians, even atheists, have experiences both exceptional and mundane every day, all over the world. We know that many people refrain from drinking for many reasons, other than a belief in God. Of course, many people in the world drink as part of a religious or spiritual tradition.

I think it's long past time to start asking why there is so much fear and prejudice, specifically toward atheists and agnostics—even in an organization like AA, which (on the surface, at least) claims to have no religious affiliation.

If a person at a meeting is going through a tough time and happens to be a believer, the mood of the meeting tends to be encouraging. However, if a person is going through a tough time and admits he's a nonbeliever, the mood becomes one of blame, as if he's met some form of punishment. I think it's time to start calling this accepted prejudice against nonbelievers by its true name: bigotry.

I've heard the cliché many times that AA is a "spiritual program, not a religious one," but if AA literature and attending over 2,000 meetings in western New York have proven one thing to me, it's that AA tends to have a strong Christian influence.

I've heard many an AA member give his or her testament of love and appreciation for a Christian God (sometimes, even Jesus specifically), oftentimes to the rapture and applause of fellow members. I have also witnessed the outright castigation of those who speak about their uncertainty, doubt, skepticism, or nonbelief in matters religious or spiritual. I have seen the same members, who trumpet their own "right" to speak about their personal understanding of spiritual matters, become hostile toward those who share a non-Christian or atheist view.

As a member of AA, I believe that this is a "we" program. "We" have a problem. "We" can't claim to love and include everyone who wants to stop drinking—and then make that love conditional on the acceptance of spiritual beliefs, especially when the only spiritual choice presented in our literature is nothing but a thinly veiled Christian idiom.

You can't really love something you don't understand. Quite honestly, that's my reason for not believing in God. I've read and listened to many passionate and erudite believers, and I've yet to come across an explanation of a divine, supernatural being that makes sense to me.

Don't get me wrong, though. I definitely agree that in times of pain or desperation, it helps to visualize an image of strength, love or beauty in the mind's eye. Different people may call that image by different names. I simply believe that our visualizations emanate from within the human psyche, an obscure dimension but not a supernatural one.

I love a number of people who are Christian. Because of my upbringing, I understand the basis of their beliefs and I am respectful of their opinions ... to the exact extent they are respectful of mine.

Conversely, it's easy for a person to become frightened, or even hostile, toward that which is unknown. Whether you were raised a believer or not, try asking yourself this question: Does my faith (or, lack thereof) afford me the courage to put aside my fears for the opportunity of understanding something different?

Anonymous

Without a Higher Power
January 2010

This atheist "walked into our midst," and stayed. At the age of 52, I attended my very first AA meeting on Oct. 7, 2001. I have not found it necessary to take a single drink since. Were it not for AA it's likely I would never have put together one continuous week of sobriety.

Finding all the "God stuff" in the Twelve Steps a bit hard to swallow, I immediately latched onto Tradition Three, which states, "The only requirement for A.A. membership is a desire to stop drinking."

I also had the good fortune of stumbling across a Twelve Step study during my first week of recovery. It has been my home group ever since. That was where someone drew my attention to the chapter on Step Two in the "Twelve and Twelve" where it states, "First, Alcoholics Anonymous does not demand that you believe anything. All of its Twelve Steps are but suggestions."

I also learned in my home group about a fellow called "Ed" in the essay on Tradition Three in the "Twelve and Twelve." His real name was Jimmy B. One of the pioneering members of the New York group, Jimmy B. was apparently the first diehard atheist to find lasting recovery in AA. His personal story eventually made it into the Second Edition of the Big Book as "The Vicious Cycle." An internet search turns up lots of interesting information about Jim. He is my personal AA hero.

Eventually I also discovered the pamphlet "Questions & Answers on Sponsorship" where, much to my relief, it points out that "some alcoholics have been able to achieve and maintain sobriety without any belief in a personal Higher Power." That includes me.

In an article published in the April 1961 edition of Grapevine (reprinted in *The Best of Bill*), Bill W. laments: "Though 300,000 have recovered in the last 25 years, maybe half a million more have walked into our midst, and then out again ... . We can't well content ourselves with the view that all these recovery failures were entirely the fault of the newcomers themselves. Perhaps a great many didn't receive the kind and amount of sponsorship they so sorely needed."

I certainly know what that's like! I ended up firing two sponsors in my first three months of recovery. The first one dogmatically insisted that I absolutely had to turn my will and my life over to the care of some kind of Higher Power if I wanted to stay sober long. My second sponsor relapsed.

Unfortunately, sponsors who actually follow the excellent suggestions outlined in "Questions & Answers on Sponsorship" seem to be about as rare as four-leaf clovers. I ended up without a sponsor for 15 months before hooking up with my current sponsor. By then I had made a lot of progress working a personalized program of recovery I had designed for myself, one that makes absolutely no reference to any kind of "Higher Power" concept—not even using my home group or AA as a whole as a substitute for God. My new sponsor's first official advice to me was, "Whatever you've been doing is obviously working well for you, so let's not try to 'fix' it."

After years of studying the Twelve Steps in my home group and discussing them with my sponsor, I now understand why faith in "God *as we understood Him*" was so vitally important to Bill W. and most of the AA pioneers.

As clearly explained by Dr. Harry Tiebout in the appendix of the book *Alcoholics Anonymous Comes of Age*, they nearly all suffered from some form of narcissism. Their narcissism had effectively blocked their recovery from alcoholism and eventually turned them into low-bottom drunks of the "hopeless variety."

The obvious cure for rampant narcissism and grandiosity is greater humility; and as it says in the essay on Step Seven in the "Twelve and Twelve," "the attainment of greater humility is the foundation principle of each of AA's Twelve Steps."

However, as Dr. Silkworth points out in "The Doctor's Opinion," "The classification of alcoholics seems most difficult." Ultimately, he tells us, all alcoholics "have one symptom in common: they cannot start drinking without developing the phenomenon of craving." That certainly describes me. All of us do have issues of our own that we need to deal with if we are to stay both sober and happy, often issues that "the attainment of greater humility" simply will not touch.

The program of recovery I work directly addresses my issues. The only person in the world it needs to work for is me, and it does that very, very well. Today I am not only sober, I am far happier than I had ever dreamed it was possible for me to be.

I now have a dozen sponsees of my own. Four of them, like me, are atheists who have absolutely no use for the Higher Power concept. Two of those have already enjoyed over four years of continuous sobriety.

Obviously I do not insist that my sponsees must all work the same program of recovery, nor do I tutor them in the program of recovery I designed to address my own issues—"defects of character," if you wish. Instead, I encourage each of them to follow my example by identifying their own issues, and then working a deliberate, systematic, active program of recovery designed by themselves, for themselves, to directly address their issues.

Over the years I have endured a lot of criticism from other AAs for my unorthodox beliefs, especially for my refusal to endorse the Twelve Steps as a perfect one-size-fits-all program of recovery for every alcoholic. But if Bill W. were alive today, I'm sure he would approve. As he suggested in the long form of Tradition Three, "Our membership ought to include all who suffer from alcoholism. Hence we may refuse none who wish to recover."

That certainly includes me. My fondest hope is that if enough others follow my example, someday it will include millions more like me who previously might have "walked into our midst, and then out again."

Greg H.
San Diego, California

Is "Agnostic" a Nasty Word?
September 1969

I t seems to me that the word "agnostic" is too often abused and the diversity of agnostic ideas too little understood by individuals, both in writing for AA publications and in speaking at meetings. Frequently, the writer or speaker will describe an atheistic point of view and label it agnostic. Not stopping with this practice, he will then proceed to use the word "agnostic" in a derogatory sense.

I wonder where some of our AA members get the notion that an agnostic believes in nothing. Even the atheist may have a personal creed, a Higher Power. However, it is not my intention to speak for the atheists—they speak for themselves.

As an agnostic, I do not accept as ultimate truth the theological explanations of what God is or isn't. My disbelief in ancient theological lore, if it is taken literally, doesn't make me less the believer in the ultimate existence of good in mankind.

We don't know what electricity is, but it would be no less a force by another name or no name at all. Because it has certain physical properties, mankind accepts it as a physical phenomenon. There was a time when intelligent people thought quite differently. Then, it took an agnostic temperament to disbelieve that deities were exercising their supernatural powers in the form of bolts of lightning, and this skepticism paved the way to more enlightened thinking on the subject. If, throughout the history of man, old ideas concerning deities had not been thrown out at the prompting of agnostic thinking, modern culture would not exist and the AA program could not have covered the broad spectrum of human relationships that it does cover and will continue to cover.

Because of his views, the agnostic isn't fettered with fear of supernatural punishment or expectation of reward for good behavior. He is free to explore the theologies of mankind without feeling he must subscribe to all those varied viewpoints in order to appreciate their spiritual beauty. The agnostic seeks. He does, intuitively, recognize the Something in his life, yet he doesn't fit it into the cut-and-dried concepts of any theology. He is looking just as deeply and experiencing life just as profoundly as those who profess an orthodox belief.

The agnostic's temperament fairly hums with unorthodox ideas. His search for proof is inherent in his nature. He is not just being antisocial or stubborn in his seeming reluctance to formulate or accept a theological deity. He knows there is Something, but he doesn't name it, define it, nor confine it to any theology; his inner convictions do not permit him to be satisfied with defining his spiritual experience in theological lingo. He is totally unable to deny that summons within himself that causes him to seek enlightened answers inside the realm of his own understanding and inner experience.

During my nine years of sobriety in AA, I have spent a reasonable amount of time trying to understand the difference between agnostics, like myself, and orthodox believers concerning spiritual experiences or enlightenment. I have studied the written experiences of Christianity's more famous personalities who underwent seemingly dramatic inner change, and I have listened to the inner conflicts expressed by my fellow agnostics while they were undergoing deep inner change. Frankly, I don't see an appreciable difference in the phenomena of spiritual awakening and its development encountered by certain mystics of Christendom and by enlightened agnostics in AA. The differences that do exist are only in the varying ways of formulating the experience into meaningful statements. The orthodox believer calls it God and employs the various techniques of theology in reasoning out the experience. The agnostic recognizes the experience to be above the level of human knowledge and therefore finds the language of man inadequate to describe the wonder and awe he feels when he undergoes deep inner change or enlightenment. He calls it his Higher Power. (For simplicity's sake, I have confined these comments to orthodox believers and agnostics—I am not unaware of the variety of spiritual experience that abounds in AA members of all creeds.)

Spiritual growth and experiences are not limited to orthodox believers in a deity, any more than the disease of alcoholism is limited to skid-row bums. I am sickened, at times, over the stigmatization of the agnostic. Some individuals within our Fellowship hardly realize the damaging effect their obtuse views inflict upon the agnostic newcomer. His unorthodox behavior as a practicing alcoholic has already removed him from the family of man. He knows he needs help, and it is enough that he has suffered the horrors and stigma of being a practicing alcoholic; he ought not be stigmatized in AA because he is an agnostic.

Agnostics should arouse the same respect for the dignity of their personal concepts as those who work toward the good of mankind through orthodox beliefs—both in AA and outside AA.

In the final analysis, the individual's achievement and continued maintenance of healthy sobriety are dependent upon his recognition of a Power greater than himself. Whether he personifies it in a deity or understands it as a dynamic force, it is nevertheless a Power for good, greater than he, commanding respect from all men and giving comfort, strength and joy to those who seek it.

J. B.
Casper, Wyoming

Grapevine Online Exclusive
What Are the Requirements?
October 2013

Sometimes, it seems that the Third Tradition has been amended to "The only requirement for membership is a desire to stop drinking and a belief in God." In many meetings, as well as Grapevine articles, I hear that unless I profess a belief in God, I am doomed to drink again. This God is usually not a God of my understanding but a God of their understanding.

I have been sober in AA for well over 30 years. For the first 10 years or so, I tried to believe and I made believe that I believed. At my sponsor's suggestion, I prayed daily and worked the Steps. The more I studied religion and God, the more convinced I became that this was not for me. Yet I continued going to meetings, sponsoring others (if they believed in God I did nothing to discourage them) and engaging in service work, and I stayed sober.

I find most AA literature on this subject very condescending. Even chapter four of the Big Book, "We Agnostics," promotes the idea that atheists and agnostics will eventually come to believe in God.

Discretion has become the better part of valor for this atheist at meetings. Many AAs will insist that this is a spiritual program and then go on to explain their religious beliefs and why I should accept them.

Convincing them to become an atheist is not my job or intent. While it is not appropriate for me to point out the errors of their thinking, why do they think it is their responsibility to convert me? I have no problem in believing in many powers greater than myself. I just believe in one less God than they do.

In the June 2013 Grapevine, "K.K." wrote, "Tradition Six reminds us to be careful not to endorse." When a newcomer or a visitor comes to an AA meeting and experiences it being closed with the Lord's Prayer, wouldn't they assume that, since this is a Christian prayer and AA endorses it, therefore AA must be a Christian organization? We say, "I want the hand of AA always to be there." Are we placing restrictions on who will be allowed to grasp that hand?

Bob L.
Gilbertsville, Pennsylvania

Closet Atheist
April 1978

Twenty-seven years ago, I called AA. I told the girl who answered that I had a problem.

"What's your problem, alcohol?" she asked.

"Of course," I answered, "but I'm an atheist."

She said just the right words: "Oh, that's all right; we have lots of atheists in AA."

To run me off, all she would have needed to say was, "Aw, you're not an atheist; surely you believe in some kind of a higher power."

This was a while back, when AA was smaller, and she may have passed the word that there was going to be a new man, and let's take it easy on the spiritual. In any event, not much in the way of God was stressed at the early meetings I attended.

A little background on me. I was intensely interested in the Scopes "Monkey" Trial in Tennessee in 1925. For a few years afterward, the newspapers and Sunday supplements were filled with articles on the "missing link." I began to read Darwin, Wallace, Lamarck, Mendel. In the 1930s, I joined with other freethinkers in New York City in speaking on atheism. A group of us picketed a radio station in San Francisco, demanding (successfully) that an atheist be allowed equal time on Sunday. So much for background.

The Twelve Steps appeared to mean what they said. The members told me that I could use any concept of a higher power I liked. In Step Two, maybe it makes sense to believe that the power which is to restore my sanity is the power of the group, and in Step Three, maybe the group could do something with me if I turned my will and my life over to it. But it didn't make much sense to me. Then came Step Five. How do I admit my shortcomings to a God or something I do not believe in? Six and Seven required some mental skirmishing. I concluded, within eight or nine months, that if I couldn't reconcile my beliefs, I couldn't stay sober in the program.

Since I had been a Catholic in my youth, I went to the church for instruction. For nine months, once and sometimes twice a week, a priest labored with me, explaining Genesis. I argued Darwin to him. After nine months, he (and I) thought I now believed in God and the theory of creation. Because of a series of marriages and divorces, the church allowed me to attend Mass, but not to take the sacraments. This made me a sort of second-class Catholic. Talk about resentments!

But I stayed sober. For five years. Then I blew it. After a short stay on skid-row and with the help of Goodwill, I got back uptown and back on the program. I recently celebrated my 20th AA birthday.

I think what keeps me sober more than anything else is the AA Preamble: "Alcoholics Anonymous is a fellowship of men and women who share their experience, strength and hope with each other that they may solve their common problem ..." That, I can buy, and I do buy it.

I'm a "closet atheist." I join in the Lord's Prayer, knowing it doesn't harm me, any more than it harms a Catholic to add "for Thine is the kingdom, etc." When any spiritual question is under discussion, I usually pass when called upon to speak. I don't proselytize inside or outside of AA; I'm not trying to convert anyone to my way of thinking. I'd just ask some well-meaning, enthusiastic members not to come down so hard on the God question. There are atheists in them there foxholes; there are atheists in AA.

So let's have a little tolerance—tolerance perhaps of the unexpressed secret beliefs of the person next to you. We'll never know why that new member didn't come back. It's unpopular to be an atheist, and not every atheist admits it openly. So let's not run the agnostic or the rationalist off, back to the world of drinking.

I'm glad they didn't run me off!

C. C.
Sacramento, California

CHAPTER FOUR

Group Life

Participation in service is a key component of sobriety
for many members

An AA group is often defined by its basic inclusivity and the understanding throughout the Fellowship, as stated by Bill W., that "Any two or three alcoholics gathered together for sobriety may call themselves an AA Group." Participation in the life of a group is open to all AAs and many atheists, agnostics and nonbelievers have found service within the Fellowship to be a great avenue to recovery.

"I've done a lot of service work of every kind in my time in AA," writes Life J. in his story "Open-minded," "and I know many other agnostics—with double-digit time in this program—who, like me, have dedicated themselves more to doing service than the average member."

In "An Atheist Lets Go," Gene J. writes about starting a new meeting for atheists and agnostics and becoming its GSR—before he even knew what a GSR was. "I got the service bug, you might say," when he realized that his clubhouse didn't have a meeting for atheists and agnostics. Someone suggested he start one—and he did.

One alcoholic helping another is the basic building block of AA and, as Jerry S. writes in "Finding Our Way," even in finally admitting to himself that he didn't believe in God, he discovered there was one thing he did believe in without reservation: AA. "AA works because only an alcoholic trying to stay sober can help another alcoholic wanting to get sober. ... And the bonding that can occur between them is a spiritual experience! ... That, I believe, is what really happened in Akron between Bill and Dr. Bob, and it is still how it works today."

Coincidently Sober
October 2016

Once someone posted on their social media page, "GOD EXISTS." I felt compelled to reply, "Where's your proof?" The response back was, "Coincidences—there are too many to be accidental." My reply was, "I guess I just haven't experienced enough to be convinced."

I have experienced coincidences since I started in AA. The first one occurred when I opened a meeting directory, after finally admitting to myself that I had a problem and needed help. I found a meeting called We Agnostics, located directly across the street from the liquor store that I would walk to at night when I wanted more booze. It was at that meeting that I was able to find a sponsor who I was fairly certain would not be forcing God down my throat. The mere fact that a meeting called We Agnostics existed gave me hope.

The next coincidence occurred after I had read a bit of AA literature. I became concerned about whether I'd be able to stay sober for the long haul since I find it impossible to believe in a god. Would the Fellowship as a Higher Power be enough? That's when a Grapevine magazine arrived in the mail (via a subscription that I had—coincidentally—won in a raffle). In that Grapevine was an article that mentioned a woman who had remained sober for 40 years using the Fellowship as her Higher Power. Forty years! I was relieved to know that indeed you can be an atheist and stay sober for the long haul, that atheism is not a barrier to sobriety.

And here's another coincidence: I volunteered to become a General Services Representative (GSR) for my We Agnostics home group with the hope that I could figure out how I could advocate for the creation of a pamphlet aimed at alcoholics who had a problem with the preponderance of God in AA literature. And the very first GSR-related event I attended was a "Concepts" workshop. And on one of the tables there was a pamphlet titled, "Many Paths to Spirituality," which was pretty much everything that I would have advocated for.

Now, if I were one of those folks who believed that coincidences are proof of the existence of God, I would be thinking that God was OK with me being an atheist. I believe God just wants me to get sober, whether I believe in him or not. But since I'm not one who believes that coincidences prove God exists, I'm thinking that the reason there was an agnostic meeting, the reason there was a Grapevine article and the reason there was a pamphlet is because enough frustrated atheist and agnostic members in AA spoke up. And I am so grateful they did because I probably wouldn't be here if they hadn't.

S. B.
Ventura, California

Open-minded
October 2016

I got sober, initially on my own, on February 20, 1988. But I realized after a couple of months that it would only be a matter of time before I would drink again if I didn't get some help, and since I was close to broke, AA was the only option.

I knew only a little about AA, and certainly all the god stuff was a surprise, but I stayed. I think I stayed because at my second or third meeting I got to sit next to this really big guy who talked about being scared of people, and that was something I could relate to. I was scared of people too. This guy probably saved my life, and he will never know it. I felt like I'd come home, in spite of the god stuff, and AA has been my home until just a couple of years ago. I still come several times a week, though it doesn't feel like home the way it used to.

I never made a secret of being an agnostic, or perhaps an atheist; it doesn't much matter to me what we call it. But I also didn't find much reason to talk a whole lot about it.

Then about six or seven years ago, I found myself attending online AA rooms, and there I would often see newcomers getting badgered with a need to find a god, until they left in a cloud of protests and disgust. I did not have it out with the old-timers who did it, but it made me more and more uncomfortable. I then stumbled upon the group AA Agnostica, and I got quite involved there. One day a newcomer walked into our local fellowship and announced that she was an agnostic. I decided then and there it was time to start a meeting for unbelievers. So I started collecting materials, and then went to our local intergroup and announced that I was going to start a freethinkers' AA group. I figured no one would have a problem with it. It was, after all, liberal Northern California, right? But though there seemed to be a small favorable majority, it was put up for discussion for the following meeting whether this meeting could be listed in the schedule—even though it says on the schedules that meetings are listed at their own request and that it doesn't constitute endorsement. A couple of people were especially against it, and started gathering the votes against it. I held out bravely, but eventually gave up the fight 14 months later.

This whole experience radicalized me way more than I ever wanted to be. I would much rather have been left to just go about my business, focus on my recovery, help the few agnostic newcomers who come my way, along with helping any other newcomer that I can, and have us all be one big happy family. But it feels like the unity has now been lost for the sake of top-down uniformity.

These days, I find myself antagonized by any mention of god, at least to the extent it is presumed to be on my behalf too. And I'm aware that there is considerable support for this uniformity from a number of other intergroups and individual members around the country that have decided to start governing AA. The book *Daily Reflections* is forever a thorn in my side now. It is read at the beginning of many AA meetings, and it seems like no matter what the beginning quote is, it ends up being a talk about god. And as the *Daily Reflections* go on and on about it, so do I. I'm sure there will be old-timers who say that it's just because I have only been sober for 28 years, and more will be revealed.

On the other hand, one agnostic, 43 years sober, finally came out of the closet after I started talking about it. She had been hiding very cautiously all those years. At some point I may settle back down, but it sure doesn't feel like it. I fear that the "more" that will be revealed is how AA is becoming ever more fundamentalist in spite of the fact that people with "none" for a religion are on the rise in the general population, the general population is on the rise, and AA is shrinking. We need to get back to open-mindedness, love and tolerance if AA is to not eventually shrink into becoming a quaint relic from the last century, or just one more obscure religious movement.

There needs to be room for unbelievers in AA, instead of them just sitting on their hands in meetings while members talk endlessly about god. Unbelievers should be fully appreciated members of AA, with everything we have to offer. I've done a lot of service work of every kind in my time in AA, and I now know many other agnostics—with double-digit time in this program—who, like me, have dedicated themselves more to doing service than the average member.

I do want to say that I've been rewarded with a good life. AA saved my life, no doubt about it. However, I just no longer have this fuzzy feeling that I'm part of the tribe, though there are a few open-minded believers who go out of their way to try to make me still feel part of.

Bill W. always stressed inclusivity, and as he got older and his sobriety matured, he got to be ever more open-minded about agnostics in AA. We did start our Freethinkers' Group, in spite of not being listed, and I have to announce it everywhere I go. Intergroup, our new governing body, wants to keep us out, yet our meeting falls way, way inside the following parameters outlined by Bill W. in Grapevine in 1946, when he was 11 years sober:

"Any two or three alcoholics gathered together for sobriety may call themselves an AA Group. This clearly implies that an alcoholic is a member if he says so; that we can't deny him his membership; that we can't demand from him a cent; that we can't force our beliefs or practices upon him; that he may flout everything we stand for and still be a member. In fact, our Tradition carries the principle of independence for the individual to such an apparently fantastic length that, so long as there is the slightest interest in sobriety, the most unmoral, the most anti-social, the most critical alcoholic may gather about him a few kindred spirits and announce to us that a new Alcoholics Anonymous Group has been formed. Anti-God, anti-medicine, anti-our recovery program, even anti-each other—these rampant individuals are still an AA group if they think so!"

Life J.
California

An Atheist Lets Go
June 1998

Years ago, when I first began to play with the idea that I might be an alcoholic, I spoke with a few people who were members of AA hoping to gain an insight into my problem. But with each person I spoke to I ran into a roadblock in the form of the Second and Third Steps. The usual message I received was that it was all right to be an atheist as long as I believed in God. Neat trick.

I tried to point out the contradiction in this idea but I was told that I couldn't work the AA program without some sort of higher power, whether I called that higher power God or something else. "Why not use a chair as your higher power?" they'd tell me. (For some reason they always used a chair as an example.) I had two problems with this suggestion. First, it was an insult to my intelligence. Second, I wondered just what kind of concept of God they had if they relegated God to the status of a Lazy-Boy lounger.

At the time, I was seeing a counselor who was trying to get me into AA. She thought there was an atheist group somewhere in town but she wasn't sure where. I decided that if there was a higher power he didn't want me to join AA. If he did, he would have created a group that denied his existence!

I was hospitalized for about seven weeks for depression. Though my alcoholism wasn't treated, I was able to give it some serious thought while I was there. I left the hospital accepting the fact that I was an alcoholic but not knowing what to do about it. I rejoined a therapy group I'd belonged to. The very insightful counselor who facilitated that group had dug up information on a special interest AA group for atheists and agnostics. He knew that my only rational defense against joining AA was my atheism, so when he gave me this meeting information I decided I was going to check it out.

I won't go into detail about how nervous I was at that first meeting or how everyone welcomed me and made me feel comfortable, not only with my alcoholism but with my atheism as well. Knowing they'd been through the same thing made me stay.

My first four months in AA were exclusively at this meeting. I couldn't imagine attending traditional meetings. But as time went on I began to feel more secure in my feelings and was encouraged to attend "God meetings" occasionally. My first such meeting was at the local clubhouse, and it was on the Fourth Step.

Good, I thought, I won't have to deal with the Second and Third Steps. And I didn't. Obviously, by admitting I was an alcoholic, I had completed my First Step, so now all I had to do was just concentrate on the Fourth Step. (Actually I was going to concentrate on how to avoid the Fourth Step—but that's another story.) But the concept behind the Third Step was still a problem for me.

I'd always been a willful and manipulative person. I pulled my first con job at the age of three. I developed this little song and dance that not only made my family adore me but also allowed me to turn them against my older brother. But I was now beginning to see that my days as a star were over. I had no job, no money and no home. I was living in a shelter, picking up cigarette butts out of the gutter, believing that I had no future at all.

Since I didn't have a higher power to turn my will over to, I decided to just let my will go in any direction. It didn't matter where it ended up, I just wanted to get rid of it. Maybe I could make other people take responsibility for my actions, so I started doing everything people told me to do. I followed every suggestion in an almost zombie-like fashion. And there was never a shortage of advice.

"Don't drink," I was told. No sweat. I didn't have money for booze anyway.

"Go to meetings," they'd say. No problem. It was better than hanging around the Salvation Army center with all the crazies.

"Listen to what is said at meetings." I had no choice. I was a zombie.

At first the things I heard went in one ear and out the other. But then something amazing happened. They began staying in my head. Good grief!—the things I was hearing began making sense. Things about honesty, integrity and fellowship. Promises about serenity, intuition and security.

Security? I was getting a little worried about my security. I mentioned to my first sponsor that the shelter would be closing in a week and I had no place to go. He said, "Mention it at a meeting. Someone might respond." Good advice. I mentioned it at a meeting and someone not only offered me a place to stay for a while but a temporary job to boot, helping him work on his house. It turned out to be ideal. He lived only two blocks away from the clubhouse so I was able to go to as many meetings as I wanted.

Since the job was temporary, I knew I'd have to look for another one. Once again I employed my sponsor's suggestion. At one of the special interest meetings I casually mentioned that I'd soon be looking for a job as a legal secretary. A woman handed me a business card. Two days later I had a good job with a prestigious law firm.

The same thing happened with my apartment. Someone suggested I check the bulletin board. I found a business card on the board for an apartment building. I was only planning to stay there until the end of summer until I could find a decent place to live, but I ended up liking it so much I'm staying for a year.

Then there was my involvement with the atheists and agnostics group. I got the service bug, you might say, so when I realized that the clubhouse didn't have a meeting for atheists and agnostics, someone said I should start one, which I did. A friend said I should become the new meeting's GSR. I took his suggestion and became the GSR. I got so enthusiastic about this new position that a week later I even asked my friend what a GSR was. He told me, but I realized that it was too late to back out.

I notice that there are a lot of people who approach the Third Step from what I think is the wrong perspective. They spend their time try-ing to find this "God they understand" in order to turn their will over to him/her, not realizing that there doesn't have to be a recipient of their will: all they have to do is let it go. And that's what I did, I let it go.

Here's Step Three as it might be read for those who believe as I do:

"Made a decision to entrust our wills and our lives to the care of the collective wisdom and resources of those who have searched before us."

That "collective wisdom" taught me so much. But the most impor-tant thing is this: when we give up our will we don't give up our re-sponsibility. And though I'm starting to gain more control over my own life, I still listen to, trust and follow the advice I get from that collective wisdom.

But I'm past my initial year of sobriety, and I know I have to accept the responsibility of becoming part of that collective wisdom. And I have to be ready for someone else to drop his will into my lap, some-one who's going to trust me. I know that as long as I don't forget the advice I was given, I can't possibly give bad advice to someone else.

So I'd like to end by giving some advice to all of you. Take a break, have some coffee and just turn it over.

Gene J.
Chicago, Illinois

A Larger Welcome

(From *Dear Grapevine*)

November 1996

During the 1996 General Service Conference, the Southeast New York Area recommended that a pamphlet be created for the alcoholic who is a nonbeliever. Unfortunately, the Conference's decision was to not consider the idea for a pamphlet.

I know that AA is a spiritual program, and not necessarily a religious one, but sometimes the distinction is not always clear. I've read the chapter "We Agnostics" in the Big Book, but found that it wasn't very reassuring to a newcomer who hadn't found God. In the beginning, I was afraid that if I couldn't (or wouldn't) believe in God, I wouldn't be able to stay sober. This is terrifying to a new member.

Of course, many new members don't even read the Big Book. That's why I believe that the concept of AA pamphlets evolved. And even though there's an AA pamphlet entitled "Do You Think You're Different?" the other "differences" mentioned in the pamphlet now have individual pamphlets devoted to those concerns—all except the atheist/agnostic. Why?

I wonder how many alcoholics are lost to AA because they can't or won't believe in God. I've spoken to many sober alcoholics who tell me that even though they did eventually find a Higher Power of their understanding, as beginners they had a real hard time with the "God thing." Many went out to do more research. How many have never returned? In the We Agnostics Group of New York City, for which I'm GSR, we hear many such stories.

I wish that the time had come to consider a larger welcome to those drunks who have an initial or ongoing dilemma with the concept of a

Higher Power. I hope we can all remember that our program is one of inclusion, and that it's incumbent on all of us to welcome anyone who walks in our doors, no matter what they believe.

Naomi D.
New York, New York

A Few Words From an Atheist
April 1985

I dried out, sobered up and found peace by becoming aware of, then learning to be grateful for, the simple things that make up the joy of living, instead of wallowing around in the exact nature of my wrongs; by letting others help me help myself, instead of searching for moral supremacy; by learning to live and let live; and certainly not by examining someone else's "wrong" thinking about God, the Big Book, or the Twelve Steps.

Serenity has not been granted me by divine intervention or by waiting for it to land in my lap. Serenity, along with such goodies as a sense of belonging, a newfound freedom and happiness, and a better understanding of myself, comes my way by the learning of acceptance. Acceptance, especially, of the simple fact that some people believe in God and some do not.

There is a very real human power called sharing, without which I would not be alive today, let alone relieved from alcoholism today.

That's the way it works for me, and I'm willing to let it.

J. A.
Dayton, Ohio

My Search
October 2016

I came to my first AA meeting by accident, sort of. I was there to support a best friend in high school who was sober. I had been dabbling in drinking with some pain but I wasn't at my bottom—yet.

At that first meeting, the seed was planted when an AA member said, "It's not how often you drink or how much you drink. It's what happens when you drink." In response, I told myself that I was only a weekend binge drinker and was only 16. But a few months later, I hit an emotional bottom with painful repercussions. I knew exactly where to go because this time I was ready. I had lived that member's foreshadowing statement.

I came to AA desperate and incredibly green to anything Twelve Step-related. I took all suggestions, no questions asked. When spirituality arose, I did what was suggested to me and conceived my own Higher Power to the best of my ability. I used the group itself as my Higher Power for quite some time, along with my deceased great-grandmother and nature.

Someone suggested I pray and develop conscious contact with my Higher Power. But I never felt a genuine connection to this idea, though my ears perked up when fellow members talked about God. I hoped I could take what they were doing and incorporate that into my spiritual repertoire.

For five years, I tried "fake it till you make it." My impression was that if I didn't have a Higher Power, I would drink again. The fear of that notion kept me earnestly and enviously searching for what everyone else seemed to already have. I didn't tell anyone I was struggling to come to some understanding of a Higher Power. I didn't ask anyone whether I could stay sober without a conception of one. Also, I had a wonderful sponsor who believed, and I felt that because I didn't, I had failed.

Then the day came when a fellow member and friend was open about his atheism. I was intrigued and honestly awestruck that it was acceptable to be both sober and atheist. That day was the beginning of an alternate route of spirituality for me. I learned that the best thing I could do was to continue to search, question and investigate. Eventually I came to the realization that I'm an agnostic and have been my entire life. I needed to be true to myself because I was feeling increasingly different in a room full of people who I needed to feel connected to.

The Fellowship around me embraced me wholeheartedly. My sponsor then stopped suggesting prayer and saying things like, "Let go and let God." We started together figuring out what spiritual tools would work best for me. In meetings, I began speaking openly about my view and letting others know that it's OK to honestly let people know where you're at spiritually. We all need to be open-minded to others' ideas. We need to be honest and willing to change.

I've met opposition for my beliefs. I've also had people have the utmost gratitude to know they're not alone and that we can stay sober regardless of what we believe or don't believe. I've sponsored Buddhists, Christians, agnostics and those who are in the process of discovering. I still have a sponsor who believes in God. For me, the beauty of sobriety is that I can learn from everyone and anyone.

I've had the pleasure of helping like-minded AA members start a group—the first in our area—that my friend the atheist calls We Agnostics. It's a meeting where people can express themselves freely. We just had our one-year anniversary. It's amazing to see the growth the group has had and to feel the growth it has provided me. I have the gift of getting sober young and the pleasure of helping others be true to themselves. I couldn't ask for anything more.

Cara A.
St. Peters, Missouri

Finding Our Way
October 2012

After being in and around the AA program for more than 30 years, I now have 17 years of continuous sobriety. I was not able to get sober and stay sober until I became honest with myself about "the God thing."

Religion and church attendance had been a significant part of my early life. We lived across the street from the Methodist church that my grandfather had helped establish, and I attended Sunday school regularly. I frequently attended church with my grandfather and became a member when I was 12.

In junior high school I was introduced to the sciences and adopted them as my sources for understanding the world and myself. Math and the sciences were my primary focus in high school, and I majored in mechanical engineering in college. Church attendance was only at Christmas and Easter, if I went at all.

With marriage and children, church again seemed the thing to do. We joined a Methodist church, enrolled the kids in Sunday school and began attending regularly. For me, it became just a good way to kill an hour until sports programming started on TV and the convenience stores could sell beer. When the kids were old enough to have the option of not going, we reverted to Christmas and Easter attendance. Asked if I believed in God, I could truthfully answer, "Yes." However, I viewed the Bible as no more than a collection of legends and fables, and religious practices as having some benefit, but holding no real significance for me.

There was nothing unusual about my drinking history—for an alcoholic. From a few beers in high school, my drinking progressed until alcohol took control of my life. Finally, largely thanks to my doctor's (a neighbor) and wife's nagging, I consented "to do something about my drinking." My doctor identified several treatment options, and I selected the one that sounded most compatible with my lifestyle. That I might be an alcoholic never entered my mind. I didn't fit the profile, I thought. They put me in the backseat of our car with a six-pack of beer, and off we went. After a brief interview, I was admitted on the spot.

It was a total surprise to me that the treatment program turned out to be very AA-oriented. In addition to AA meetings held at the facility, we were transported to two or three other meetings a week, so I received a good introduction to the program.

When I was discharged, I was given a list of AA meetings in my small city. I started attending a couple of meetings a week and performing minor service work, but mostly just sat as an observer. The only thing I was doing right was not drinking, but I was a long way from being sober. That lasted a little over two years. Then I drank for four months and returned to the program after a brief "rehab refresher."

Convinced that I had to get more serious, I started following directions. I read the Big Book, memorized its prayers and recited them in my morning meditations. I joined a group and got a sponsor, studied the "Twelve and Twelve" and worked the Steps. I attended at least five meetings a week, and did service work in my home group. Feeling good about my progress, I was confident my sobriety was solid.

Eight years later, domestic and job-related problems arose and I got drunk. After 11 weeks of drinking, I went back to the program totally demoralized. I was sure I had learned my lesson. A little over two years later, I got drunk again.

Feeling that I must be one of those "hopeless drunks," I immediately started going to AA meetings again, but there was something very wrong. If asked, I could still honestly say that I believed in God, but God had no real meaning for me.

I stayed in and around the program for several months, but nagging questions kept haunting me. Was I constitutionally incapable of being honest with myself? What is it about AA that works, when the best theological and medical minds have tried for centuries to find a solution? Why would a loving God wait until Mother's Day, 1935, to plant the seed that grew into the AA program when alcoholism has been a problem for thousands of years? What was it about that meeting between Bill W. and Dr. Bob that was so special?

All I knew for certain was that something had to change or I was going to start drinking again. In desperation, I finally got honest about "the God thing." Only to myself at first, I admitted that I did not believe in God. That was the lowest point of my life. I was not drinking, but now I did not feel comfortable in AA either.

Fortunately, I realized there was one thing I did believe without reservation: AA works! In all those years in and around the program, I had seen too many "drunks" get sober—and stay sober. So, if there is no God, why does it work? I have found my answer, one that enables me to stay sober. AA works because only an alcoholic trying to stay sober can help another alcoholic wanting to get sober. It works because only a recovering alcoholic can identify with, have credibility with, and thus help another drunk. And the bonding that can occur between them is a spiritual experience! They help each other stay sober. That, I believe, is what really happened in Akron between Bill and Dr. Bob, and it is still how it works today.

We need to remember that AA, with or without God, does not cure us of our addiction to alcohol. If we were truly "cured," wouldn't we be able to drink normally? AA gives us the hope, the will and the tools to live without drinking—but only for one day at a time. It gives us a philosophy and the support for living a life that is healthy, happy, joyous and free. That does seem like a miracle, especially to a suffering alcoholic.

There are now six freethinkers' meetings a week in our city. It started with the We Agnostics Group and three or four drunks showing up. Today, we have three groups meeting in different parts of the city and often have over 20 recovering drunks in attendance. We continue to grow in membership and in acceptance in the greater AA community. Our meetings follow the usual formats: we have both open discussion and literature study (Big Book and "Twelve and Twelve") meetings.

The main difference is that there are no prayers. We read Appendix II from the Big Book at the beginning of our meetings and close by reciting the AA Responsibility Declaration: "I am responsible. When anyone, anywhere, reaches out for help, I want the hand of AA always to be there. And for that: I am responsible."

There are freethinkers' groups all over the country with increasing numbers of sober agnostic and atheist drunks, proving that there is a choice. In working with newcomers, we stick to the basics and encourage them to work the Steps, but also to find their own understanding of a "power greater than themselves."

So, to all AAs, please judge us freethinkers by the quality of our sobriety. We are not trying to tell anyone not to believe in God. What we do believe in is working for us.

Jerry S.
Austin, Texas

CHAPTER FIVE

One Big Tent

In AA, we are one

Unity is one of AA's most cherished principles and, guided by the recognition that if we don't stick together as a Fellowship we are likely to die alone, members with all kinds of different beliefs work together every day for sobriety.

For some members who have accepted who they are, with their own truth, it isn't easy. AA's Steps and Traditions urge us to strive for tolerance and unity.

"Everyone contributes in this unique and special Fellowship," writes Eddie B. in his story "Practice, But Don't Preach." "We are guided by principles greater than each person which protect the sanctity of each of us and allow us to come together to do what we could not do alone."

Adds Ward Ewing, Class A (nonalcoholic) former trustee of AA's General Service Board in his essay "We Share Common Ground," "This Fellowship has always found unity through love and tolerance, not theological agreement."

In "An Unsuspected Inner Resource," member Dan H. writes, "I have been sober nearly 28 years now, and I still can't say much about a God 'out there,' one that created the universe. ... I have, however, had a deep and effective spiritual experience as a result of the AA Steps bringing me into contact with 'an unsuspected inner resource.' ... If someone asks, I might just say that there's something inside of me that's smarter and kinder than I am, and I think I'll listen to it."

Writes Frank B. in "One Big Tent," "There is nothing in the word God that frightens or offends me, at least not anymore. I know that when I use the word, it may have a different meaning than when my fellows say it. I have no problem with that. I am so grateful that AA is a big tent with room for everyone."

Can an Atheist Find a Place in AA?
June 1964

As I read Grapevine every month, one thought always stands out in my mind. Many stories are about particular alcoholics who have found their niches in life and, more important, in AA. In each case, there is a fight, a surrender and an acceptance. This seems to be topped off by an air of enthusiasm about the Fellowship, and a tranquility about these individuals which is almost an entity unto itself.

Here is a new approach to AA, or here is how some of the other half lives, the half made up of scared-to-death newcomers, "doubting Thomases" and me, the outright nonbeliever who finds that certain words in the English language still have their mysterious power over the chemical forces in the body. The mere mention of them makes me want to be physically ill. Some of these dandies are: acceptance, society, conformity, God, religion and at times, even the word alcoholic.

Joshua Loth Liebman once said that "Agnostics are like the damned spirits of Dante's inferno, condemned to be whirled forever on the shifting winds of opinions and emotions, and that atheism at bottom means the inability of a man to utter an all embracing 'Yea' to existence. It is the denial of meaning in life, it is the distrust of the universe."

I am an alcoholic, and I am also an atheist, and it is to my own kind that I am writing—the atheist, the agnostic, the people who are still searching. A terrible restlessness pounds at our hearts and our consciences as we continue the ever-loving search for what's beyond the next green hill, with the terrible realization that, above all, the first drink is out.

For as shocking as this may seem to some people, I am one of those individuals who do not enjoy being an alcoholic, and I know that there are many more like me. I also know that this is contrary to all the basic laws of staying sober, which brings the number one point in question to the test.

Can such a person find his place in AA? And if he can, how does he manage to stay sober? I tried AA in 1960 and after one meeting and one particular slogan that kept glaring at me to the bitter end, But for the Grace of God, I went out and got drunk, and stayed drunk for another year—a year filled with horror and degradation that in comparison made my other nine years of drinking seem like kid's play.

Having had my fill of people and life, and people and life having had their fill of me, I again turned to the last door that was open to me: AA, and to that slogan that I dreaded so much the year before.

The first night back, I don't think I would have cared if God Himself had been the chairman. I was staying, and I have stayed, and if the prisoners don't get too restless upstairs in my overactive mind, which I think of as Cell Block 9, I will be staying every day, each and every 24 hours of them one at a time.

I believe that there is a place in the world and in AA for people who do not have the capacity to believe, and that we are no more or no greater oddballs than those people who do believe. After all, faith is not something that you can buy packaged and ready for sale in a grocery store. You either believe or you don't believe, and if you don't, stop worrying about it. You can still stay sober. I have been around AA a few 24 hours, and when I received my two-year medallion, I was convinced that there is a place in AA for you and me.

They say, "Don't fight it." I try not to, but there are many times when I still do. I can see that beautiful pot of gold at the end of the rainbow, but so often I have stumbled and fallen, and mentally slipped back. It is foolish to run; I can barely walk.

There is an old proverb that says "A journey of a thousand miles begins with the first step." Today, Step One is behind me on my road to glory and continued sobriety.

If, in my travels and search for truth on this twisted, hazardous road of life, I chance to meet the one they call God, my secret wish is that we will recognize each other and that pride will not keep me from accepting and admitting the painful truth, when and if I do find it. On the other hand, should I not meet any strangers on my journey, I will be contented and happy in my realization that AA as my higher power is walking close behind as I continue one step at a time toward that pot of gold at the end of my rainbow, which is filled with every one of my diamond-studded 24 hours of sobriety.

Is there a God or isn't there? I say it doesn't matter. Keep an open mind and don't give up the fight because of a slogan or someone's personal credo. The highway is wide enough for all of us, and the rules for pedestrians are: Keep an Open Mind; Keep Coming Back.

Anonymous

Practice, But Don't Preach
April 1994

Bill W. warned of the spiritual pride that would delude us into thinking we had a direct pipeline with our Higher Power: "In AA's first years, I all but ruined the whole undertaking with this sort of unconscious arrogance. God as I understood him had to be for everybody. Sometimes my aggression was subtle and sometimes it was crude. But either way it was damaging—perhaps fatally so—to numbers of nonbelievers." Bill reminded us (and me too) that "we ourselves need to practice what we preach—and forget the 'preaching,' too."

I need to be reminded constantly that I don't have all the answers just because I consider myself spiritually fit, and that the greatest example of false pride and self-righteousness is to claim, "I have the answers!" That is what divides us from cults and religions: No one person speaks for the Fellowship; each member can have a power greater than themselves or not; and the only requirement for membership is a desire to stop drinking. There is no requirement for anyone to believe as I do. We are each allowed to accept or reject what we wish—and that is the great power and beauty and attraction of this program.

In a 1940 letter, Bill W. stated that "we make no religious requirement of anyone ... In such an atmosphere the orthodox, the unorthodox, and the unbeliever mix happily and usefully together. An opportunity for spiritual growth is open to all." Everyone contributes in this unique and special Fellowship. We are guided by principles greater than each person which protect the sanctity of each of us and allow us to come together to do what we could not do alone. We understand, as Bill W. eventually did, that each person's theology has to be his own quest.

Today I've learned tolerance and understanding of those who have an orthodox belief in the cosmos; some need a more structured belief system than others. I've learned to forgive those who turn meetings into testimonials and remind me of my old church days. I try to not judge those who judge me for not having a Higher Power called God, or because I don't pray the Lord's Prayer at the end of a meeting. I think it's in conflict with the Sixth Tradition of our Fellowship. The Lord's Prayer comes from the Bible, and if that ain't endorsing Christianity, I don't know what is. I'm just grateful I don't retaliate and end a group with a Buddhist chant.

This is a spiritual, not a religious program. Let's keep it that way. I won't force my beliefs on you if you don't force yours on me. Say what you want, and so will I with the help of my Higher Power whom I choose not to call God, and together we'll stay sober one day at a time.

Eddie B.
Ahwahnee, California

We Share Common Ground
October 2016

Ward B. Ewing is a past chair (Class A, nonalcoholic) of the AA General Service Board (2009-2013). He is an ordained Episcopal priest and a past president of The General Theological Seminary in New York City. — The Editors

In November of 2014, I was privileged to participate in the First International Conference for Atheists, Agnostics, and Freethinkers in AA. Many seemed surprised that I, as a religious, nonalcoholic person whose spiritual life has been strengthened, sustained and enriched by this Fellowship, would be part of this group. Frankly, I was surprised by the exclusion from AA felt by many of the participants in the conference. I knew about areas where the intergroups had "delisted" groups because they self-identified as being for those who cannot accept belief in a transcendent deity, but I was unaware of the depth of pain experienced by so many who were told they could never stay sober unless they came to believe in a God of their understanding. Clearly that conclusion is not true, as I met many with 30 or 40 years' sobriety who do not believe in "an anthropomorphic, interventionist (male) deity." As one participant expressed his experience, "You would be surprised by the scrutiny (be it reality or perception) that nonbelievers are subject to within AA at large. Some of our fellow AA members are fearful, dismissive or outright hostile toward us."

I was surprised because atheists and agnostics have been a part of AA from the beginning and even played a role in writing the Big Book. Opinions of those uncomfortable with traditional God language led to the change in the Steps shortly before it was published. In Step Two the term "God" was replaced with "Power greater than ourselves," and in Steps Three and Eleven the term "God as we understand Him" was used. And the Steps are clearly identified as suggestions (in *A.A. Comes of Age*).

As we all know, membership in AA is defined by the Third Tradition, "The only requirement for A.A. membership is a desire to stop drinking." We have a single primary purpose articulated in the Fifth Tradition, "to carry [the] message to the alcoholic who still suffers." Part of what has always been an attraction of AA for me has been its openness to anyone who desires to stop drinking. Before other organizations were open to African-Americans (and other minorities), women, or gay and lesbian persons, AA welcomed them. This record of inclusion is dramatic, and comes from the Third Tradition. I do not understand how anyone might be excluded because of theology. Intolerance born of religious certainty is as old as the hills and as destructive and ugly today as it has been in the past. This Fellowship has always found unity through love and tolerance, not theological agreement.

We often hear stories of people who were turned off by the God-talk when they attended their first AA meeting. They returned because they had no place else to go. Many later found a God of their understanding that supported their new life. We do not, however, hear the stories of those who were turned off by the God-talk at their first meeting and who never returned to AA. One can only fear they never found help.

I have previously written about the importance of maintaining the distinction between religion and spirituality ("Spirituality & 'God-Talk'," Grapevine, April, 2010). AA is a spiritual program; it is not religious. Religion has a way of sneaking in, and when it does, we run the risk of excluding some who come seeking help and are turned off by religious language. Some never come back. I recognize that each group is autonomous, but I find I am uncomfortable with religious language, particularly in open meetings.

As Bill W. wrote in Grapevine in July 1965: "Newcomers are approaching AA at the rate often of thousands yearly. They represent almost every belief and attitude imaginable. We have atheists and agnostics. We have people of nearly every race, culture and religion. In AA we are supposed to be bound together in the kinship of a common suffering. Consequently, the full individual liberty to practice any creed or principle or therapy whatever should be a first consideration for us all. Let us not, therefore, pressure anyone with our individual or even our collective views. Let us instead accord each other the respect and love that is due to every human being as he tries to make his way toward the light. Let us always try to be inclusive rather than exclusive; let us remember that each alcoholic among us is a member of AA, so long as he or she declares."

The spirituality of the Twelve Steps and of AA as a whole is clear and powerful. Hope, truth, honesty, letting go, acceptance, loving others as a way of loving self, gratitude—these are spiritual realities that are part of the culture of AA. One might also mention unity, carrying the message, singleness of purpose, self-support and anonymity as spiritual characteristics. These qualities form an invisible, intangible culture; they are spiritual realities. They are difficult, maybe even impossible to define; we must experience them. Just so are lives changed and formed by this invisible culture, this spirit of AA, that is an integral part of the Fellowship. This is experiential spirituality. It is pragmatic. It is known through living, not from some preordained theoretical position. What truly matters is this spirituality: a newcomer caught by hope, the sharing of one's story seeking above all to be truthful, letting go of the desire to be self-directed by choosing a sponsor, identifying with another who is both different and yet the same, discovering the gifts we have been given, becoming happy, joyous and free—all made possible by the spirit of AA—unseen, indescribable, known through experience.

I find that believers, nonbelievers, theists, atheists, agnostics, and freethinkers all share common ground found in a common experience that is shaped and formed by this culture of AA. This collective power of AA is greater than any particular person or group; it makes the impossible possible. This power can be discovered within a person, but it is also beyond. It is an inner resource; it is a collective power.

Many in AA refer to this invisible reality, this culture, this spirit, this higher power as God. Others who cannot bring themselves to compromise their rational understandings to believe in some sort of deity still experience the power of this invisible reality within AA groups. I would suggest that since all the members of the Fellowship are influenced by this invisible power, the differences between those who wish to call it God and those who choose a different name are tiny in comparison to our shared experience. What we believe about something is far less important to living than what we experience. Experience is what transforms us; belief is our attempt to explain; experience trumps explanation. I believe the dialogue between those who are religious and those who are freethinkers, agnostics and atheists in AA can bear much fruit. And I believe the common ground of experience provides the basis for that conversation. I am grateful for those who share their stories in this issue of Grapevine. May we all grow from their stories.

Ward B. Ewing
Trustee Emeritus

Equal Time for Atheists
(From *Dear Grapevine*)
September 1976

I do not believe in God, but I would not change a single item in the Twelve suggested Steps or the Twelve Traditions. I call only for equal footing with other alcoholics in terms of sharing my strength and hope within the boundaries of the AA program.

For me, our common faith lies in our understanding of our relations to one another and the values contained in these human relations. Here are, in the nonbelievers circle, all the elements for a faith that shall not be confined to sect, denomination, politics, organization, institution, class, race or god. We who are now alive are parts of a humanity that extends into the remote past, a humanity that has interacted with nature. The things in our alcoholic community we prize are not ourselves. They exist by grace of the doings and sufferings of the continuous human strivings to become healthy, productive members of our community, in which we are a link.

Such a faith has, for this nonbeliever, always been implicitly the common faith of mankind, and the decision rests with his ability to take himself, his life and his happiness seriously. For me, when ties to the "magic supernatural helper" are severed, it becomes clearer and clearer that the human condition remains the most interesting, important, challenging and promising one on this, our earth.

J. MCG.
Forest Hills, New York

Open-minded
December 2013

"The phrase 'God as we understand him' is perhaps the most important expression to be found in our whole AA vocabulary. Within the compass of these five significant words there can be included every kind and degree of faith, together with the positive assurance that each of us may choose his own."
God As We Understand Him: The Dilemma of No Faith
—*Bill W., April 1961*

As I've grown older in AA, I've had to resist the urge to grow set in my ways and become close-minded about differing viewpoints. When the above quote appeared in my inbox as the Grapevine Quote of the Day, it reminded me that Bill grew in the opposite direction, and that the lifetime course of his writings challenges me to do likewise. As a young man, Bill wrote the first draft of the Steps using the narrower language "God" and strongly emphasized his "hot flash" spiritual experience in writing the Big Book. As he grew older, he became more and more accepting, urging members throughout the '50s and '60s that the best thing they could do for AA was to "raise the bottom."

Viewed against the backdrop of the phrase "God as we understand him," Bill's idea of raising the bottom far surpasses the emotional, physical, material and spiritual bottom where I became willing to consider the Fellowship of the Last Resort as an alternative to my former self-driven life as an active alcoholic. More broadly, raising the bottom challenges me today to open the door all the way, so any alcoholic can enter, dwell and remain comfortable for as long as he or she needs, regardless of the flavor or intensity of personal spiritual taste. Who am I to judge whether an agnostic, an atheist or any other kind of theist or deist, possesses the spiritual basics needed for recovery?

Once upon a time, "spiritual diversity" sounded to me like a New Age watering down of "true religion." Now, I recognize spiritual diversity as so much healthier than its alternative—which would be spiritual inbreeding. If I can't trust my Higher Power to protect AA from any ill effects that might arise from diversity of spiritual experience among our members, then I don't have much of a Higher Power, do I?

B.C.
New Market, Maryland

An Unsuspected Inner Resource
February 2016

What if there is no God?

This question has haunted me periodically throughout my sobriety. If my sobriety depends on belief in and access to a power greater than myself, what happens if there is no God?

Some say I can use a doorknob or a lamppost or anything for a God, but I don't think so. How can I turn my life and will over to a doorknob? How can a lamppost remove the character defects that the Big Book says will lead me back to drinking?

What about using the group as my Higher Power? Well, that's great, except that when I reached one year of sobriety, I found the power of the Fellowship alone insufficient. I felt depressed and indifferent to life and I mainly wanted to sleep. The group was great, mostly, as long as I was at a meeting, but it wasn't very portable, and I needed something to sustain me between meetings.

I was dissatisfied with the Big Book chapter on the subject. I felt that "We Agnostics" was a classic bait-and-switch. "Our own conception ..." morphed quickly into the traditional view of God, with all the attendant masculine pronouns and biblical implications. And yet I was sold on the idea that, on my own, I was in deep trouble.

Two phrases in the book rang true for me. The first was "something at work in a human heart ..." This was something I could work with. And then, thank God (ha!), there was the appendix on "Spiritual Experience," which mentions "an unsuspected inner resource which they presently identify with their own conception of a power greater than themselves."

I have been sober nearly 28 years now, and I still can't say much about a God "out there," one that created the universe, involves itself in natural events or dispenses the occasional convenient parking spot on a lucky day.

I have, however, had a deep and effective spiritual experience as a result of the AA Steps bringing me into contact with "an unsuspected inner resource" (which I call God as a matter of convenience). If someone asks, I might just say that there's something inside of me that's smarter and kinder than I am, and I think I'll listen to it.

It is easy enough to give alcoholism a personality: it's cunning, baffling and powerful. It is patient, doesn't discriminate and it wants to kill me. It's tied up in a tangle of knots with my selfishness, pride and fear. So it seems reasonable to personify the other side, the "place" within from which emanates love, honesty, compassion, sanity and a willingness to help others. And it seems reasonable to appeal to this place—to state a willingness to live my life under its guidance. I call this appeal "prayer."

I like to read "other books," as mentioned in the Eleventh Step. I read about religion, philosophy, science and skepticism, as well as faith. I haven't rejoined the debate society. I just enjoy exploring ideas.

An old-timer once told me that "religion is a finger pointing at the moon." What that tells me is that if I spend too much time staring at the finger I will forever miss the moon. I am no longer so interested in labels like "atheism," "agnosticism," "deism" or "theism." And I can't afford to revert to "me-ism." When I'm the center of the universe, it's a dark and lonely place.

My small God might seem insufficient to some, but it works for me. And I believe that same inner resource is a part of each of us. When I'm in a room full of people talking about God's effect on their lives, it becomes a presence that we can all sense even as our individual concepts vary.

Occasionally, I have the intuitive sense that my unsuspected inner resource is an expression of something much larger, and that perhaps there is a deeper relationship between consciousness and external reality than simply that of observer to observed.

The poet William Blake said that "the road of excess leads to the palace of wisdom." I'm still looking for that palace.

Dan H.
Oceanside, California

One Big Tent
January 2016

I got to the rooms of AA in April of 1980, and as is the case with so many of us, I had no belief in God. More than that, I was positively hostile to any suggestion that there was a God and that he had any particular interest in me or my problems. None of my God beliefs made any difference in my belief in the AA program though. I don't know where that belief came from, but I knew I was where I belonged. This AA thing would work for me.

For many years I struggled with "the God thing." I don't think it threatened my sobriety, but I felt out of step and did not want to keep feeling that way. A couple of years ago I was reading the story "Flooded With Feeling" in the Big Book. The last few paragraphs reflected my own feelings and left me with a huge sense of relief. The thunderbolt—"Who are you to say there is no God?" in the chapter "We Agnostics" had a different effect on me than on the writer. It did not convince me that there is a God, but it relieved me of the necessity to doubt that there was one.

Also, two stories in the February 2013 Grapevine especially rang true for me: "One Dark Night" and "That Big Green Thing" were written to let me know that I am definitely not alone.

There is no doubt in my mind that the Big Book definition of "a Power greater than ourselves" is, for me, God. That's OK with me now. I believe there are many powers greater than me, and I'm fine with calling any or all of them God today.

There is nothing in the word God that frightens or offends me, at least not anymore. I know that when I use the word, it may have a different meaning than when my fellows say it. I have no problem with that. I am so grateful that AA is a big tent with room for everyone.

Frank B.
Mesa, Arizona

No Worshipping For Me
October 2016

work a secular program, omitting the religious aspect (as I see it) of AA philosophy. Try as I could, "acting as if" just did not cut it for me. I was being untruthful. The power greater than myself that restored my sanity was death. I did not want to die at age 35 and it was going to happen if I did not change direction.

I do not worship the Big Book. I read it as literature, documenting what the early AAs thought and did to stay sober. Similarly, the Steps are a guide to sobriety. The word "miracle" is not part of my vocabulary. I believe we dismiss our ability to grow and change when we use this word. Hard work, dedication and emotional growth are part of my language. I do not think that divine intervention occurs when a member loses the desire to self-destruct via alcohol any more than when they relapse. The Serenity Prayer works fine for me as a vital tool for living. Never having been on my knees to say the Third Step or the Seventh Step Prayers, I am sober and happy nonetheless.

My personal payback occurs when I answer the phones at our intergroup office or make copies of tapes or CDs to give away to members. Payback also occurs when I go to speak, sponsor an alcoholic, or simply attend and share at meetings. If I did not go to meetings at age 80, how would any newcomer know that the program works for me?

In a sea of many religious AA members, it's often lonely being secular, but I have to remember that without AA I would be dead. I owe my life to this program and the many sober members I've met and interacted with for all these 45 years.

Marnin M.
Hobe Sound, Florida

Spiritual Honesty

(From *Dear Grapevine*)
December 2007

Though I had searched my entire life, I never identified with a deity. I tried to accept what others believed, but always felt I was in a masquerade. When I sobered up, I wanted so desperately to have the peace and serenity that I saw on those sober faces that I would have believed in anything.

My solution was to share with my sponsor, then with a trusted friend, then finally, in a meeting. What I shared was this: My personal Higher Power is the collective spirit of humankind—if humans put their heads and hearts together, they can achieve anything.

Blasphemy to some, peace for me. My concern was how my beliefs would affect a young woman who had asked me to sponsor her. I realized that honesty in all things would be my path.

I feel no resentment toward the few who try to persuade me that I am lost, or that some particular religious figure is the answer. I love AA and do not feel excluded by others' faiths.

AA brought me sobriety, love, joy, sorrow and acceptance. More importantly, AA brought me to a true understanding of myself and a power greater than myself—the untiring and persevering spirit of humankind.

Mary E.
Sherman, Texas

God On Every Page
October 2016

Recently I visited a relative in Maine who asked me only one question about AA: "Is it religious?" My first thought was, Of course it is. Instead I paused, and told her she had asked the $64,000 question.

I thought back to that bleak day 10 years ago when I washed up into AA, still a bit tipsy, beaten into a state of reasonableness and literally dying to find a way out of my alcoholic addiction. As my head cleared, I started reading the Big Book, and since the word God seemed to be on almost every page, I thought I had to return to the Christianity I was raised under in order to get sober.

I soon realized our book didn't actually say I had to return to the God of my youth. But I felt it strongly implied that those who really got the program and stayed sober eventually returned to their faith in good old American fundamentalist Christianity. I was so depressed. I'd never fit in with these people, I thought.

Fortunately I found a wonderful sponsor, a born-again Christian no less, who was instrumental in taking me through the Steps, including the God parts, and showed me how I could find a new way of living free from that hopeless state of mind and body I had dragged into AA with me.

We read the Big Book side-by-side, often rereading "We Agnostics" and the Appendix II on spiritual experience. He said that if I didn't have the power myself to stop drinking and manage my life, I'd have to rely on some other power that did. The main thing was that power had to be greater than me.

We discussed the Oxford Group's Four Absolutes and the Buddhist's Eightfold Path. He suggested I could replace the word God with Good, or with Higher Power or Group of Drunks or Good Orderly Direction. Our book called it God, but we can call it anything we want.

Had I believed in God there would have been no problem, but I didn't. Try as I might, I could not convince myself I had an ethereal friend who would direct my will according to some predetermined life plan. So how could I get sober and stay sober without all that God stuff?

I asked those who had what I wanted if they believed in God, and if not, how they stayed sober. I was amazed at the number of people who spoke of their reliance on a truly spiritual force to stay sober, and never referred to God. They told me how they had worked through the Steps and slowly discovered that their Higher Power had nothing to do with God or religion.

As I went through the Steps, I came to believe in a higher purpose, not a higher being, to help me change the way I thought and acted. My higher purpose is to live by the principles of the Steps. The power I draw on is that unsuspected inner resource which makes me willing on a daily basis to strive for honesty, integrity, compassion, tolerance, humility, love and service. After cleaning house, sharing my faults, making restitution and starting to help others, I was relieved of my obsession to drink and much of my selfishness and self-centeredness. I became grateful for what I had and was much more comfortable in my own skin.

So how did I answer my friend's question? I told her AA is a spiritual program although many of its members are religious. I said the Big Book was not simply an instruction manual, but a historical document, and reflected the predominately religious roots and views of its early members.

Our book is not perfect, but it does try to keep the door open to atheists, agnostics, freethinkers and alcoholics from all walks of life. Today, I don't need God to have a higher purpose in my life and to practice the principles of the Steps. I simply need to believe that with help from the Fellowship and my inner resources, I can change my own attitude and actions and continue to enjoy the enormous benefit that change has brought into my life.

Alex M.
Louisville, Kentucky

The Twelve Steps

1. We admitted we were powerless over alcohol—that our lives had become unmanageable.
2. Came to believe that a Power greater than ourselves could restore us to sanity.
3. Made a decision to turn our will and our lives over to the care of God *as we understood Him.*
4. Made a searching and fearless moral inventory of ourselves.
5. Admitted to God, to ourselves, and to another human being the exact nature of our wrongs.
6. Were entirely ready to have God remove all these defects of character.
7. Humbly asked Him to remove our shortcomings.
8. Made a list of all persons we had harmed, and became willing to make amends to them all.
9. Made direct amends to such people wherever possible, except when to do so would injure them or others.
10. Continued to take personal inventory and when we were wrong promptly admitted it.
11. Sought through prayer and meditation to improve our conscious contact with God *as we understood Him,* praying only for knowledge of His will for us and the power to carry that out.
12. Having had a spiritual awakening as the result of these steps, we tried to carry this message to alcoholics, and to practice these principles in all our affairs.

The Twelve Traditions

1. Our common welfare should come first; personal recovery depends upon A.A. unity.
2. For our group purpose there is but one ultimate authority—a loving God as He may express Himself in our group conscience. Our leaders are but trusted servants; they do not govern.
3. The only requirement for A.A. membership is a desire to stop drinking.
4. Each group should be autonomous except in matters affecting other groups or A.A. as a whole.
5. Each group has but one primary purpose—to carry its message to the alcoholic who still suffers.
6. An A.A. group ought never endorse, finance or lend the A.A. name to any related facility or outside enterprise, lest problems of money, property and prestige divert us from our primary purpose.
7. Every A.A. group ought to be fully self-supporting, declining outside contributions.
8. Alcoholics Anonymous should remain forever nonprofessional, but our service centers may employ special workers.
9. A.A., as such, ought never be organized; but we may create service boards or committees directly responsible to those they serve.
10. Alcoholics Anonymous has no opinion on outside issues; hence the A.A. name ought never be drawn into public controversy.
11. Our public relations policy is based on attraction rather than promotion; we need always maintain personal anonymity at the level of press, radio and films.
12. Anonymity is the spiritual foundation of all our traditions, ever reminding us to place principles before personalities.

AA Grapevine

AA Grapevine is AA's international monthly journal, published continuously since its first issue in June 1944. The AA pamphlet on AA Grapevine describes its scope and purpose this way: "As an integral part of Alcoholics Anonymous since 1944, the Grapevine publishes articles that reflect the full diversity of experience and thought found within the A.A. Fellowship, as does La Viña, the bimonthly Spanish-language magazine, first published in 1996. No one viewpoint or philosophy dominates their pages, and in determining content, the editorial staff relies on the principles of the Twelve Traditions."

In addition to magazines, AA Grapevine, Inc. also produces an app, books, eBooks, audiobooks and other items. It also offers a Grapevine Online subscription, which includes: new stories weekly, AudioGrapevine (the audio version of the magazine), the Grapevine Story Archive and the current issue of Grapevine and La Viña in HTML format. For more information on AA Grapevine, or to subscribe to any of these, please visit the magazine's website at www.aagrapevine.org or write to:

AA Grapevine, Inc.
475 Riverside Drive
New York, NY 10115

Alcoholics Anonymous

AA's program of recovery is fully set forth in its basic text, *Alcoholics Anonymous* (commonly known as the Big Book), now in its Fourth Edition, as well as in *Twelve Steps and Twelve Traditions, Living Sober,* and other books. Information on AA can also be found on AA's website at www.aa.org, or by writing to:

Alcoholics Anonymous
Box 459
Grand Central Station
New York, NY 10163

For local resources, check your local telephone directory under "Alcoholics Anonymous." Four pamphlets, "This is A.A.," "Is A.A. For You?," "44 Questions," and "A Newcomer Asks" are also available from AA.